"Too often, the stories of faithful Black women have been lost to history. Thankfully, Jasmine Holmes has done the hard work of bringing these stories to light by chasing down footnotes and searching through archives for her new book, *Carved in Ebony*. Reading these stories will encourage your faith, inspire your courage, and remind you of God's extraordinary work in the midst of the everyday faithfulness of his people."

—Melissa Kruger, author and director of women's initiatives
for The Gospel Coalition

"*Carved in Ebony*, like its author, is courageous, compassionate, and clear. In considering the lives and faith of the women profiled here, we can learn how we as Christians can serve Christ and love the world for which he died and lives again."

—Russell Moore, public theologian at *Christianity Today*
and director of *Christianity Today*'s Public Theology Project

"Jasmine Holmes dusts off the lives of ten Black women in history, placing their contributions to the world and the Church squarely in our current climate and circumstances. I was convicted, comforted, and challenged by Jasmine's strong, wise, and informed voice. *Carved in Ebony* is a treasure that belongs on every shelf of American history."

—Lore Ferguson Wilbert, author of *Handle with Care: How
Jesus Redeems the Power of Touch in Life and Ministry*

"Jasmine Holmes has uncovered a wealth of buried treasures in the lives of these remarkable, inspiring, and ordinary women. They have so much to teach us today, and we have so much to learn. Get ready to be humbled and awed by these powerful Black women."

—Karen Swallow Prior, research professor of English and
Christianity and Culture at Southeastern Baptist Theological
Seminary and author of *On Reading Well: Finding
the Good Life through Great Books*

"I can recommend *Carved in Ebony* for so many reasons: its serious historical research, its vivid writing, its unflagging commitment to the Gospel, its challenge to lasting racial prejudice. But let me say it most plainly. The stories of these ten Black women inspire faithfulness and courage. They offer a glimpse of what God can do when we surrender ourselves to him."

—Jen Pollock Michel, author of *A Habit Called Faith*
and *Surprised by Paradox*

"*Carved in Ebony* introduces the stories of Black women that for too long have been untold. With unapologetic conviction and vulnerable eloquence, Jasmine shows how their faith and *steadfast purposefulness* indelibly shaped our nation and world. You will be both inspired and challenged to continue the legacy these women began."

—Elizabeth Woodson, institute classes
and curriculum director, The Village Church

"What a gift this book you hold in your hands will be to you! Jasmine has a way of teaching you a history lesson you never knew you needed, while also pointing you to a God who deeply cares for his children. I love God more now that I know these ladies in this book, and I suspect you will as well!"

—Jamie Ivey, bestselling author and host
of *The Happy Hour with Jamie Ivey* podcast

"Books are meant to shape us. While reading *Carved in Ebony*, I imagined that I was joining Jasmine Holmes on a journey looking at old truths with fresh eyes. After I was done, I realized that Jasmine wasn't just using her pen to tell a story. She was using it as a chisel. My faith and confidence in the goodness of God has been refined and polished as a result of seeing God's faithfulness in the lives of these women. I can't wait to witness the other statues she sculpts when other people get their hands on this book."

—John Onwuchekwa, pastor of Cornerstone Church
and cofounder of Portrait Coffee

Carved in Ebony

LESSONS FROM THE BLACK WOMEN WHO SHAPE US

Jasmine L. Holmes

BETHANYHOUSE

a division of Baker Publishing Group
Minneapolis, Minnesota

Published by Bethany House Publishers
11400 Hampshire Avenue South
Minneapolis, Minnesota 55438
www.bethanyhouse.com

Bethany House Publishers is a division of
Baker Publishing Group, Grand Rapids, Michigan

Printed in the United States of America

Library of Congress Cataloging-in-Publication Data
Names: Holmes, Jasmine L., author.
Title: Carved in ebony : lessons from the black women who shape us / Jasmine L. Holmes.
Description: Minneapolis, MN : Bethany House Publishers, a division of Baker Publishing Group, [2021] | Includes bibliographical references.
Identifiers: LCCN 2021028776 | ISBN 9780764239700 (casebound) | ISBN 9780764238857 (paperback) | ISBN 9781493433711 (ebook)
Subjects: LCSH: African American Christians—Biography. | Christian Women—United States—Biography. | African American women—Religion. | African American women—Religious life. | Women and religion—United States—History. | United States—Religion.
Classification: LCC BR563.N4 H6545 2021 | DDC 277.3008996073—dc23
LC record available at https://lccn.loc.gov/2021028776

Cover art and design by Jena Holliday

Author represented by The Gates Group

Baker Publishing Group publications use paper produced from sustainable forestry practices and post-consumer waste whenever possible.

21 22 23 24 25 26 27   7 6 5 4 3 2 1

For the Black women who shape me
Mommy—Bridget
Mama—Ophelia
and Ma—Karen

Contents

Foreword

Ebony.

Stubborn. Unyielding. Commodified. Precious.

The ebony tree is most often found standing alone on a vast savanna, defying harsh elements that would wither other vegetation.

She survives and grows because her Planter watches over her solitude with love and careful attention.

As she matures, she receives a hundred years of sunlight and rich earth nourishment, and stretches her limbs toward the nighttime stars.

When the Planter becomes Woodsman, she is suddenly felled. Though her fall to the ground is hard and resounding, her Woodsman is no harsh plunderer. He only earnestly desires to fashion her ebony trunk into the eternal, priceless commodity he intended from her seed-hood.

Once fallen, her nature is still stubborn and unyielding, except in the hands of the expert Craftsman who has now brought her to his side.

He leaves off his large cutting tools and moves to fine carving, excising unnecessary pieces to reveal what he sees inside her roughhewn trunk. He shapes her edges, softening some and leaving others intentionally sharp for the moment they are used for her good and his glory.

The Craftsman leans in close for this detailed work, eye and hand anticipating every nick, dark curl, and plunging wave—intention and love guiding his precision. As he polishes with his cloth, his creation drinks deep of his nourishing holy oil. A million crisscrossed hues unveil from within her darkness, uncovering the Master's splendor that he knew lay deep within.

Jasmine Holmes is herself a work of the Master Craftsman, and she has unearthed ten completed works of art: women from American history who were likewise "carved in ebony" and yielded to their Creator. She gives voice to the particular struggles and kingdom victories of pioneering, self-sacrificing Black female missionaries, and celebrates God's glory in their lives and his kingdom advance in their respective spheres.

In this volume, Mrs. Holmes has flipped our vision to see as God sees. As we arrive at the final words of her last chapter, we regard as wise what the world called foolish; what the world regarded as unremarkable, God's purpose has made most noteworthy; and what the world called weak, we now see as strong.

Carved in Ebony captures many truths, but this one rings: left to grow wildly on our own, we all remain as stubborn, unyielding, and vulnerable as the ebony tree. Yet the Master Craftsman sees what each is to be, and longs for us to be pliable in his hands. He anoints his own with the oil of the Spirit, and we in turn may reveal his splendor and presence to a world of other solitary, precious, eternal works of art.

I'm grateful to witness the age of rediscovery, uncovering God's work in unlikely places, through unlikely people. *Carved in Ebony* is a wonderful contribution to this necessary movement, for if the truth is to be told, most of us will be remembered much like these women—faithful servants overlooked in the annals of men, but whose lasting kingdom-building deeds are recorded and rewarded by the Savior who sees, hears, and promises to remember all.

Take this moment and pray with me—right now—that many more overlooked stories of faithfulness will be uncovered and told as an encouragement to the next generations . . . perhaps even shared under the shade of an ebony tree, growing alone in a far-off land.

—K.A. Ellis, director,
Edmiston Center for the Study of the Bible and Ethnicity

Introduction

I never understood the excitement that my friends shared about reading the entire Bible in a year. In my two decades as a believer, I have tried to complete this elusive task more than once, and each time I have failed. Sometimes, I make it to the major prophets; sometimes, I stall out in Genesis. Other times, I bounce around and find solace in the Gospels and epistles; and still others, I am lost in miles of Old Testament genealogies and ceremonial laws.

The Bible is many things. It is the God-breathed Word (2 Timothy 3:16) that tells the truth of the Word who became flesh and dwelt among us (John 1:14). It holds the law, which teaches us how to live (Galatians 3:24); and it holds the Gospel, which offers us the hope of Christ's atoning sacrifice when we fall short (Romans 3:23–24).

The Bible is also a story. It weaves a tale of God's faithfulness to his people, from his first promise of a Savior in Genesis 3:15, to his providential choice of that Savior's family line in Genesis 12, to the long and winding journey of that promise's ultimate fulfillment in the person and work of Christ. And so, the Bible is also history—the history of the little nation through which God chose to bless all of the nations in the world.

Israel often retells the story of God's faithfulness to them: when Moses led them across the Red Sea—before they entered the Promised Land itself—when they stood on the precipice of captivity—while they were in exile—when they returned. Story is written into their feasts and celebrations; they are commanded to recount the story of God's faithfulness to their little nation, and they recount it with gusto. Often. And it has only been through finally—finally—reading the Bible from cover to cover in a year that I have seen the pattern of recounting over and over and over again.

We Christians also have to remind ourselves of the story of God's faithfulness to our people over and over again. Because, like Israel, we are all too easily inclined to forget.

I write this book not as an intellectual or a member of the academy, but as a storyteller. My interest in history—from the historical novels I devoured as a child to the day job I had for nine years teaching history to middle schoolers—has always flowed from my love of *story*. And I am enraptured by the story that God weaves through the people he chooses to do his work here on earth.

When the Underground Railroad was at the height of its endeavor to free the enslaved people in the United States, the imagery of Israel's rescue from slavery was often employed. Harriet Tubman herself was called Moses, after the man God chose to guide his people through the Red Sea and on their journey to the Promised Land. In some places, the story of Moses was considered so dangerous that slaves[1] were not allowed access to it. Slave owners did not want to teach the story of the God who heard the cries of his people, remembered his promise to them, and led them in a victorious march toward freedom.

But they did hear the story—not just of Israel's freedom from captivity, but of God's unfolding faithfulness toward his people. And not only did they hear the story, they took up the work of sharing that story with their children, their children's children, and the nations.

As an American, it can feel threatening to tell the entire story of God's work in this nation, particularly during these polarized times. Is it unpatriotic to shine light on America's unfaithfulness to God's Word? Is it "dwelling in the past" to keep bringing up the unsavory subject of this country's shabby record of acting in good faith toward its Black[2] residents? Should we move on from these facts, or try to paint them in a more understanding light to shield the "men of their time" from our judgment? How much retelling is *enough* retelling?

In her groundbreaking work *Caste*, Isabel Wilkerson makes a compelling argument for understanding race relations in America in years past as a sort of caste system. She writes, "Americans are loath to talk about enslavement in part because what little we know about it goes against our perception of our country as a just and enlightened nation, a beacon of democracy for the world."[3] Her statement points to the truth that, when we tell the story of America, we want to tell the uplifting version of our scrappy young nation's rise to world superpower.

We could speak in vain platitudes about equality and opportunity for all. We could tout American exceptionalism as a religious truth and a coveted birthright.

I want to offer a different perspective, though. What if, instead of putting Uncle Sam in a cape and putting Lady Liberty on a pedestal, we told the story of America as the story of God's faithfulness—and not our own? What if we took a note from the people of Israel, and every time we stood on the precipice of a defining cultural moment, we reminded ourselves of God's providential hand protecting us *in spite of* our waywardness? Our disobedience? Our forgetfulness? Our selfishness? Our avarice?

What if we put God's glory at the center of our concern for the telling of our story, and left America's glory to fend for herself?

What if, like Israel, the American church proclaimed our history from the perspective of God's goodness in spite of our folly—not from the perspective of hiding from our folly?

> What if we told the story of America as the story of God's faithfulness—not our own?

By this comparison, I don't mean to say that America is *literally* a replacement for Israel. Rather, I mean to point to the fact that, in Christ, Israel's family has been expanded to include everyone who calls on the name of Jesus. And as a nation that claims Christian roots, we have a lot to learn from God's first chosen people.

It is from this perspective that I seek to tell you the story of ten incredible Black women. I tell you about their plight in our nation not to rub America's nose in her corporate sin, but to proclaim the glory of the God who heard their cries and answered their prayers and used them mightily *in spite of* their country of origin. I tell you about their struggles and their triumphs not to elevate their Blackness, but to elevate God's grace in creating that brown skin in his image. When I tell you the story of dignified Black womanhood, I do so to combat the opposite narrative, yes, but I also do it to point to the inherent dignity and worth of women, whom God created in his image and for his glory.

God's image carved in ebony.

The first time I read those words, I felt two distinct responses: a thrill of excitement, and a tinge of wariness. The excitement came first, by a hair. I was reading about Amanda Berry Smith for the first time—evangelist, missionary, devoted wife, mother to biological children, spiritual mother to countless souls, and surrogate mother to so many beautiful brown-skinned faces at the first orphanage of its kind, dedicated to caring for Black children. The woman herself—captured in an old photograph, full lips set in determination, deep eyes steely, nose and cheekbones proudly displaying a heritage I share—looks like she was literally carved from ebony. And the beauty of the fact that the people who knew this beautiful woman best saw God's image reflected in her gives me chills.

And yet, the tinge of wariness crept in on excitement's heels. Those powerful words felt almost threatening. A flood of caveats filled my brain as I looked at Amanda Berry Smith's photograph. *It's not in the graven-image kind of way*, I could hear myself clarifying to aghast onlookers if I dared name the book you hold in your hands. I'm not suggesting that God is a woman, or a Black woman at that. God is Spirit; he doesn't have a body like a man does. I've been well catechized, I promise. I know that.

But reason quickly calmed me. Because saying that Amanda Berry Smith—or Elizabeth Freeman—or Sara G. Stanley—or Maria Fearing—or Sarah Mapps Douglass—or Nannie Helen Burroughs—or any other woman in these pages—is God's image carved in ebony isn't about carving little statues and worshiping little Black deities. It's about the imago Dei—the image of God. And the fact that, even during a time in history when their personhood was being consistently questioned and cast aside, the ten women profiled in this book staked their claim to the dignity that all of us who have been made in the image of God are due. Not only did they stake their claim to their own personal dignity—they testified to the dignity of others by ministering to fellow image-bearers for his glory and teaching the world about him.

There are so many things I could have called this book. One option came from Sojourner Truth, who, though not profiled here, testified to the personhood of Black women in her stirring speech "Ain't I a Woman?"

> Well, children, where there is so much racket there must be something out of kilter. I think that 'twixt the negroes of the South and the women at the North, all talking about rights, the white men will be in a fix pretty soon. But what's all this here talking about?
>
> That man over there says that women need to be helped into carriages, and lifted over ditches, and to have the best place everywhere. Nobody ever helps me into carriages, or over mud-puddles, or gives me any best place! And ain't I a woman? Look at me! Look at my arm! I have ploughed and planted, and gathered into barns, and no man could head me! And ain't I a woman? I could work as much and eat as much as a man—when I could get it—and bear the lash as well! And ain't I a woman? I have borne thirteen children, and seen most all sold off to slavery, and when I cried out with my mother's grief, none but Jesus heard me! And ain't I a woman?[4]

With these words, Sojourner encapsulated a truth that Malcolm X would repeat more than one hundred years later: "The most disrespected person in America is the black woman. The most unprotected person in America is the black woman. The most neglected person in America is the black woman."[5]

This enslaved woman lived in a world where Victorian notions of femininity painted white women as fragile maidens in need of protection—where they were said to be under the tender care and leadership of the men in their lives, where their virtue was supposedly a thing to be prized. She lived in a world of tightly enforced modesty, chivalry, and smelling salts, one of stiff bodices, immaculate hairdos, and rigorous social standards. But she lived in that world as a Black woman—where none of those tropes of femininity applied to her own personhood. She lived in a world not of tender leadership but of a loyalty forged in violence, forced ignorance, and systemic injustice. She lived in a world where a Black woman's strength and sexuality were commodities to be bought and sold, taken, and discarded.

But, while the stunning rhetorical ability of Sojourner Truth is always worth emulation, I didn't want to ask a question, rhetorical though it may be. I wanted to make

> Black women are made in the image of God, carved in ebony hues.

a statement, one that is not up for debate: Black women are made in the image of God. They are that image carved in ebony hues, wrought with a purpose, for his glory.

These teachers, preachers, missionaries, activists, writers, wives, sisters, and mothers have so much to teach us about what it means to be both Black and American, both woman and citizen, and overwhelmingly and through it all, Christian. Their lives hold encouragement for men and women of every tribe, tongue, and nation because their lives show the beauty of truly understanding what it means to be made in the image of God. As I've learned about each and every one of them, I've grown deeper and deeper in love with my Savior, and I pray the same for every reader. And this book is a celebration of that, yes—an unapologetic rejoicing in the fact that God chose to make each woman profiled in this book both Black and female for his glory. And it was *good*. He looked through the annals of time and chose to sew Black femaleness into the gorgeous tapestry of their identity, and he placed them emphatically in the United States. He gave them myriad gifts, talents, abilities, and callings that they used to glorify him—to proclaim his name while also proclaiming the inherent dignity he gave them when he created them. Even in the face of the hardship that has forged the story of Black womanhood in the United States, we still boast a beautiful and illustrious history of triumph, innovation, grit, and femininity.

He put them smack-dab in the middle of the story he is telling. By telling their stories, I want to praise the God who wrote them. Seeing these stories merely as an indictment of America's failings is seeing these stories as far too small. Any reflection on America's sordid history is incidental to the bigger picture of the story God is weaving: no matter the failings of a nation, his work will not be silenced. No matter the invisibility of a certain demographic, his work is never silent in the lives of those who love him.

These women—Frances Ellen Watkins Harper, Maria Stewart, Lucy Craft Laney, and others—mean so much to me as a young Black woman not because of the supremacy of blackness or Americanness, but because of the faithfulness of God. As I read each of their names, I see a testimony of God's lovingkindness, of his triumph, of the beautiful diversity he has invested into American history—a diversity that is so often overlooked.

I remember the first time I read Sojourner's speech. I was teaching in an inner-city school in Minneapolis, Minnesota, and was trying to collect a group of Black historical figures for my students to write about. I stood in front of a room full of predominately Black ninth- and tenth-grade girls and shared her words for the first time, and in their faces I saw an echo of the excitement I felt in the sharing: Black women are woven throughout the history of America, and we matter.

I *am* a woman who is both Black and American. And I stand in a long line of women who balanced those aspects of their identity with dignity and significance. I am proud to stand as the recipient of their legacies—to learn from their incredible stories. This group of women has so much to teach me. And as I strike out on a balancing act of my own, each and every one of them continues to inspire me.

I stand here as a recipient of their legacy, yes. But more than that, I stand here as a recipient of the larger legacy they are part of: the legacy of the work God is doing to spread the Gospel throughout the nations using people from every tribe, tongue, and nation. The work God is doing to claim a people for himself and to equip them for his service. He is doing that work in me—he has done this work in other women like me for a very long time.

I specifically chose to focus the biographical sketches in this book around a very short antebellum/postbellum period. I did this for a number of reasons.

First, it is a historical period I find myself most drawn to, both as a learner and a teacher. At this writing, I have just finished up teaching my ninth-graders the first semester of American history, which ended right about the time the most recent of these activists were born. I could have penned biographies about innumerable Black women across the entire history of our country, but these are the stories that mystified me most.

Second, these women stand at a fascinating historical crossroads. From Elizabeth Freeman's quest for freedom just a few years after the country's founding to Nannie Helen Burroughs's founding of a school for young Black women, all of these women stood at the precipice of American citizenship. The Civil War represents a crossroads of sorts—the transition of Black people in this country operating largely in a slave caste to their carving out what it meant to belong to society as free men and women, and full citizens.

The end of the Civil War, then, meant not just the freedom of the enslaved, but the welcoming in of full-fledged citizens who had been denied their rights as Americans up until this point in history. Even free Black people had found themselves caught in the web of double standards that would be revealed by the War Between the States.

Israel came back from exile to be given the Law again—to renew their commitment to being a nation called by God. Black America came out of the Civil War with brand-new citizenship rights they had to learn to cultivate and protect. The activity leading up to the Civil War and the careful actions afterward set the stage for what it means to be fully Black and fully American. And all of these women played a part in shaping that meaning.

This book is part biography and part memoir—part research, part love letter. I am a writer, a teacher, and a mother—a history buff insofar as it allows me to helm my middle school classrooms well. My goal in these pages is not to give you a comprehensive look at the ten lives included here, but rather to (1) give you a taste of the dynamic lives of these women and to (2) show you which parts of their stories have inspired me in my own journey toward understanding what it means to be part of the story God is telling so that (3) you are inspired to delve deeper into each of their lives to see God's handiwork and proclaim his goodness.

These women were not perfect. As with any person across the face of our history, we can find missteps and errors, faults and disagreement. But overwhelmingly, each and every one of them represents a beautiful facet of Christian womanhood that has inspired me in my own walk, and that I cannot wait to bring out for you. Where they imitated their Savior, they imitated him well. Where they fell short, his grace was sufficient for them, as it is for us.

We serve a storytelling God. Come meet him through these stories.

A Midwife at the Birth of a Nation

Elizabeth Freeman

> Any time, any time while I was a slave, if one minute's freedom had been offered to me, and I had been told I must die at the end of that minute, I would have taken it—just to stand one minute on God's airth a free woman—I would.
>
> —Elizabeth Freeman

A couple of years ago, a friend of mine posted a Facebook status that caused quite a stir: "What is your favorite thing about Black women?"

The avalanche of responses ranged from outraged "All women matter" statements to truly curious "Why are you singling out Black women?" questions to actual answers to his query. The event set off a domino effect in my brain, spawning a chapter in my last book, *Mother to Son,* and fueling the entire concept for the book you now hold in your hands.

My friend singled out Black women in his status because, historically, Black women—their strength, their femininity, and their contributions—have been overlooked in this country for decades. We could spend quite a bit of time talking about why that is and how that is—and in the forthcoming chapters, we will. But as we turn our eyes to Elizabeth Freeman, I want to tell you what one of my favorite things about Black women is: our willingness to be advocates.

For our husbands, our children, our brothers, our sisters— Black women have historically stuck our necks out. Each of the ten women in this book shows the beauty of advocacy, but it all starts with Elizabeth, who began advocating for herself, and by extension, others, at the birth of this nation.

The Double-Edged Sword

Now, the strength of Black women is a double-edged sword. It's this supposed extra-human strength that led the man referred to as the father of modern gynecology, J. Marion Sims, to perform grotesque experimental surgeries on Black women without anesthesia in the nineteenth century. It's this supposed extra-human emotional strength that causes people to think of Black women as so "tough" that we can stand up to all kinds of emotional abuse and ill-treatment.

When I talk about our strength, I don't mean an extra measure of strength other ethnicities of women do not possess. Rather, I mean the unique ways that our strength has come to bear in the history of our nation. I mean the unique measure of strength that we have had to employ to survive and thrive in a nation that began with our enslavement—the unique strength we have had to employ to birth children in a society that routinely threatened and dehumanized our families.

I don't mean Herculean physical strength or supernatural emotional strength—I mean the strength that has so often been honed as *advocacy* in our communities.

Advocacy and Motherhood

Now, as a girl who was too timid to order her own food in restaurants until I reached the age of fourteen and my mom refused to do it for me (I almost went hungry on more than one occasion because of my crippling shyness), I have not felt strong many times in my life. My journey toward embracing all that it means to be a *strong* Black woman didn't really start until the birth of my firstborn son.

In the days leading up to his birth, this timid woman learned what it meant to advocate for herself, because by advocating for myself, I was advocating for the future. In 2021, almost two hundred years after that father of gynecology decided Black women were "strong" enough to help found the practice with their unanesthetized bodies, Black women are three times more likely to die in childbirth than their white counterparts.[1] And regardless of ethnicity, childbirth is one of the most vulnerable times in a woman's life, and in giving birth, she is bringing forth the most vulnerable human being we have been called to care for.

> Regardless of ethnicity, childbirth is one of the most vulnerable times in a woman's life.

When I gave birth to my first son, that timid girl who couldn't order at restaurants had to become a fierce mama bear ready to roar her child into the world. All of my shyness disappeared as I literally mounted the birth stool, *Roots* style, and ushered my child into the world and into the waiting arms of my husband. It was the first time in my life that I ever remember feeling strong and capable—one of the moments in my life I think of whenever I reflect on my femininity. Throughout the process of pregnancy, I was able to hold on to this tiny child who lit a fire inside of me—that spark moved me to speak, and eventually taught me how to roar for my baby, and for myself.

You don't have to give birth to feel these things—that strength, that femininity, that power—at least, not literally. But figuratively, those transformative moments when we take the helm of our life and *roar*, changing its course with a force that is as feral as it is feminine, those will always remind me of birth. And that's fitting, because the first woman I'm going to share with you was a midwife.

Elizabeth Free-Woman

Elizabeth Freeman, born into slavery as Mum Bett, was the first Black woman to sue for her freedom in the state of Massachusetts in 1781. During the infancy of a country that boasted the promise of equality, she dared stake a claim to that promise herself. Her master, Colonel John Ashley, contributed to the Sheffield Declaration (a legislative document for the state of Massachusetts similar to the Declaration of Independence), which stated that "mankind in a state of nature are equal, free, and independent of each other, and have a right to the undisturbed enjoyment of their lives, their liberty and property."[2] Despite helping to pen these words, Ashley himself was a slaveholder, and Elizabeth saw through his hypocrisy. Through the aid of a lawyer friend of Ashley's, Bett held Massachusetts and Colonel Ashley accountable for the promises it had made.

> During the infancy of a country boasting the promise of equality, Elizabeth dared to stake a claim.

Historian Ben Rose observes that Elizabeth's case was "the first in which a slave gained her freedom based on the principle of general equality, rather than by proving physical abuse or wrongful enslavement, as others had done."[3] Rose continues,

> In the years leading up to the Revolutionary War, New Englanders were far more dependent on slave labor than many historians might concede. Africans stripped from the shores of their homeland became artisans and sailors in the region's rum-making and maritime industries. Later, blacks became house servants, soldiers, and field hands, and symbols of success among the lawyers, ministers and merchants who owned them.[4]

The Revolutionary War did not end until 1783, but the fledgling nation of America was working hard to become a country established by the ideals of equality. The colonial North, especially, was heavily influenced by Puritan ideals and was intent upon crafting a nation that honored its residents—even the enslaved people under their care.

History often paints a picture of the South as the only place where the enslaved were bought and sold, but the North had its hand in the trade as well. The biggest difference, though, was that in the North, the enslaved had a recourse for justice.

Elizabeth Freeman was not the first enslaved person to sue her owners. In fact, another slave of John Ashley had already sued him by the time Elizabeth took up her case. However, Elizabeth was the first enslaved woman to do so successfully, setting an important precedent for slavery in Massachusetts and, by extension, all of New England.

Elizabeth was such a skilled domestic and midwife that, even after she won her freedom, John Ashley tried to hire her back. However, she chose to be employed by Theodore Sedgwick, who helped her bring her case to court. Of Elizabeth, Sedgwick once said, "If there could be a practical refutation of the imagined superiority of our race to hers, the life and character of this woman would afford that refutation."[5]

The town of Sheffield would go on to become a hub for the Underground Railroad—a place where enslaved people who did not have the means to take their case before a court of law could take full advantage of the freedom that the Sheffield Declaration had declared: "that mankind in a state of nature are equal, free, and independent of each other, and have a right to the undisturbed enjoyment of their lives, their liberty and property."

Elizabeth's tombstone reads,

> ELIZABETH FREEMAN, also known by the name of MUM-BET died Dec. 28th 1829. Her supposed age was 85 Years. She was born a slave and remained a slave for nearly thirty years; She could neither read nor write, yet in her own sphere she had no superior or equal. She neither wasted time nor property. She never violated a trust, nor failed to perform a duty. In every situation of domestic trial, she was the most efficient helper and the tenderest friend. Good mother, farewell.[6]

Years after her death, her great-great-grandson, W.E.B. Du-Bois, sociologist, educator, scholar, and graduate of both Fisk and Harvard universities, would become one of the founders of the NAACP (National Association for the Advancement of Colored People) and founder and editor of *The Crisis* magazine. His work would become the catalyst for decades of social change in America, eventually fueling the heyday of the Civil Rights movement and continuing the social change that his great-great-grandmother began by suing for her freedom.

Include (Black) Women in the Sequel

At this writing, a recording of the Tony Award-winning Broadway show *Hamilton* has made its debut on the streaming platform Disney+. Millions of Americans have watched as an ethnically diverse cast sets the very white history of our founding fathers to hip-hop music.

In one scene, Hamilton's future sister-in-law Angelica Schuyler—played by Renée Elise Goldsberry—swishes across the stage in period dress flanked by her two sisters, Diana Ross & The Supremes style, and raps, "'We hold these truths to be self-evident, that all men are created equal.' And when I meet Thomas Jefferson, I'm 'a compel him to include *women* in the sequel!"[7]

Renée is one of several Black actresses on stage at this point, and though the Hamilton plot makes some pointed references to slavery (such as a civics lesson from a neighbor, a slaver who doesn't have to pay for labor), the systemic racism at play in the founding of our country is condemned more by the colorful casting than it is by the words of the play itself.

But Lin-Manuel Miranda's version of Angelica is, of course, on to something that Elizabeth Freeman realized as well: the Declaration of Independence claimed that all men were created equal and endowed with inalienable rights, while some of its signers withheld these rights from the men and women whom they legally owned.

It's important to note that at this time, America was still deciding what kind of nation it was going to be. Slavery, though part of the country's history for over a century at the time of Elizabeth's trial, was still hotly contested among the founders. As Katharine Gerbner points out in her book *Christian Slavery*, one of the major red flags about slavery early on was that if the colonists shared the Gospel with the enslaved, those Africans would no longer be viewed merely as "savages," but as brothers and sisters in the faith. Some owners went so far as to withhold the Gospel from their slaves, thinking that, were they baptized, they would hold a special claim to freedom.

In other parts of the world, the enslaved were permitted to read only bits and pieces of the Bible; the Bible titled *Select Parts of the Holy Bible, for the Use of the Negro Slaves, in the British West-India Islands* cut out, for instance, God's liberation of the Israelites from Egyptian slavery.

Elizabeth stood on the cusp of these decisions, providentially placed in a region that was trying to navigate the legislation of slavery with biblical principles. In 1652, for instance, Rhode Island enacted a law that limited slavery to a term of ten years, trying to imitate the year of Jubilee in the Old Testament (although, notably, this law was not long observed).

In fact, the institution of slavery was beginning to seem so tenuous in Massachusetts that when Quock Walker sued for his freedom shortly after Elizabeth Freeman did, their court cases set a precedent that would effectively topple the institution of slavery in the state during their lifetime.

Elizabeth could have borne this like the fourteen-year-old version of me at a restaurant, but instead she went the lioness-of-a-birth-giver route and demanded what was owed her according to the Massachusetts Constitution in a landmark case that changed the course of slave-owning history in the state—the results of which trickled down and changed the course of my life here in Mississippi.

This woman witnessed the birth of a nation and *took part in that birth* by staking a claim to freedom that would echo throughout generations. While the founding fathers were drafting declarations and signing documents, she was in court advocating for her freedom on the basis of those documents—and taking a bold stance for freedom for every Black person in America.

True, I am an impassioned history teacher who eats this stuff for breakfast, lunch, and dinner. It is hard for me not to make this section a dissertation on the rights of man. But one need not be a history buff to appreciate the fact that this woman—who could not even read, and would not have been allowed into the hallowed halls where decisions were being made for our country—made a decision for herself that changed the course of history. She looked at this fledgling nation and decided to become a partaker in freedoms that most people didn't think even applied to her.

It was magnificent. *She* was magnificent.

This is the kind of citizen I want to be.

A Forgotten Path to Citizenship

While many are no longer familiar with Elizabeth Freeman's case, most know a bit about Dred Scott's famous lawsuit.

Less than forty years after Elizabeth Freeman's death, America would enter into the bloodiest war in the nation's history over the very issue she contested in that courtroom. The nation would had shifted from one potentially poised to phase out slavery to one in which the southern states were fighting tooth and nail to maintain their "peculiar institution." The same nation that granted Elizabeth her freedom in 1781 would famously deny Dred Scott that freedom more than seventy years later.

> She staked a claim to freedom that would echo throughout generations.

In the mid 1800s Dred Scott sued for his freedom on the grounds that much of his servitude had been carried out in free states (states where it was illegal to hold enslaved people). In the long and grueling court proceedings that followed, echoes of Elizabeth's case seemed dim. Elizabeth had been granted her freedom sheerly based on the language in the Declaration of Independence, laying claim to the rights of citizenship that she believed her country promised all of its residents. Yet, by the time Dred Scott's case made it to the Supreme Court, those citizenship rights were as hotly contested as they ever had been.

Chief Justice Roger B. Taney clearly articulated his beliefs after the trial (emphasis mine):

> In the opinion of the court, the legislation and histories of the times, and the language used in the Declaration of Independence, show, *that neither the class of persons who had been imported as slaves, nor their descendants, whether they had become free or not, were then acknowledged as a part of the people, nor intended to be included in the general words used in that memorable instrument.*
>
> It is difficult at this day to realize the state of public opinion in relation to that unfortunate race, which prevailed in the civilized and enlightened portions of the world at the time of the Declaration of Independence, and when the Constitution of the United States was framed and adopted. But the public history of every European nation displays it in a manner too plain to be mistaken.[8]

Said another way, Justice Taney believed that the Declaration of Independence could apply only to citizens of the United States—people whose rights that Declaration was meant to protect. Taney would further argue that Black people were simply not the class of people meant to be protected by this document.

> They had for more than a century before been regarded as beings of an inferior order, and altogether unfit to associate with the white race, either in social or political relations; and so far inferior, that they had no rights which the white man was bound to respect; and that the negro might justly and lawfully be reduced to slavery for his benefit. He was bought and sold, and treated as an ordinary article of merchandise and traffic, whenever a profit could be made by it. This opinion was at that time fixed and universal in the civilized portion of the white race. It was regarded as an axiom in morals as well as in politics,

which no one thought of disputing, or supposed to be open to dispute; and men in every grade and position in society daily and habitually acted upon it in their private pursuits, as well as in matters of public concern; without doubting for a moment the correctness of this opinion.[9]

Within eighty years, enslaved people like Elizabeth Freeman had gone from being able to use the words of a document similar to the Declaration of Independence in arguing for freedom, to being considered by court opinion not to be due those rights because they were not—nor could they ever be—citizens of the country where they labored.

It is so important to put Elizabeth's actions into the context of what would take place in the nation long after she had died. Her self-advocacy was the first in a long line of steps that would reveal the blatant hypocrisy of chattel slavery's existence in the "land of the free." It would also serve to illustrate the shift of the nation from one that realized slavery could not coexist with notions of liberty and freedom to one that would fight for slavery at the cost of the Union.

What Mum Bett Taught Me

Those seeds that Elizabeth planted would sprout into a history-making legacy of advocacy. She used the knowledge at her disposal—the Sheffield Declaration—to vie for her freedom. Though not a well-educated woman because of her life circumstances, she was obviously intelligent enough to know her rights and petition for them.

This millennial has a lot to learn from her foremother on that score. If a woman who was systematically barred from education and advancement can use a snatch of a document that she overheard in conversation to stand up for her rights, what excuse do I—a twenty-first-century woman with unlimited education and information at my fingertips—have for *not* acting on my own behalf and the behalf of others?

Mum Bett is quoted as saying, "Any time, any time while I was a slave, if one minute's freedom had been offered to me, and I had been told I must die at the end of that minute, I would have taken it—just to stand one minute on God's airth a free woman—I would."[10]

Elizabeth set an important precedent through her "freedom suit." She showed, as thousands who followed after her would show, the blatant hypocrisy of a nation that claimed that freedom was a God-given right and yet denied it to many on the basis of their skin color. She held her master accountable for his abuse of power—and she won.

There is power in knowing what our founding fathers described as our "inalienable rights." Elizabeth Freeman knew them when she was petitioning for her freedom, and we would do well to know them as we inhabit our modern lives. Just a few overheard words from the Sheffield Declaration changed the course of Elizabeth's life, and history as a whole; how much more can our understanding of the wealth of words penned about our invaluable rights change our own lifetimes?

This legacy sounds intimidating when painted in such heroic strokes, but, looking at the rest of Elizabeth's life, we see that her faithfulness was lived out in the day-to-day. That court appearance was just one aspect of who she was.

Elizabeth wasn't a brilliant Civil Rights lawyer who spent her entire life advocating for legislative change. She was a domestic worker and a midwife who spent most of her time serving others and, according to her headstone, keeping her word. That part of her life—the part where she was faithful every day—is something I relate to much more than the freedom suit.

Look back at the words on her headstone: *She neither wasted time nor property. She never violated a trust, nor failed to perform a duty.*

She was a good steward of her time and her belongings. She was trustworthy. She applied herself diligently to every duty. In this sense, her advocacy for her freedom is not the defining characteristic of her life but an *outworking* of her true character. Elizabeth Freeman is not merely memorable because of her court case; rather, she is memorable because she had the type of character that made her a good steward of the freedom she had been given by God, giving her an understanding that she was not merely property. She never violated the contract that all citizens of this country pledged allegiance to, and did not neglect to perform her duty as one of the shapers of the nation that we now reside in.

Elizabeth Freeman wasn't a trailblazing activist. And yet, I believe that it was because Elizabeth herself was a woman of her word and a woman of principle that she could not sit idly by while her nation reneged on the contract that it had made with its people, including its enslaved people.

> Elizabeth's advocacy for her freedom was an outworking of her true character.

That is an example I want to follow. A woman who is faithfully about her work each and every day, but willing to step outside of that work and outside of her comfort zone to hold a nation or an individual accountable. A woman who advocates every day on a small scale—for myself, my husband, my children, my loved ones—and isn't afraid to advocate on a larger scale when the occasion calls for it.

Elizabeth's Rights

Little is known about Elizabeth Freeman outside of the details of this trial. As far as we know, in her eighty-five years on this earth, she never did learn to read or write. Would that she had learned, as her contemporary Phillis Wheatley did, to hold a pen and share her thoughts. (There can only be one Phillis Wheatley, of course, but even a journal entry would do.)

But the beautiful thing about Elizabeth's story is that, whatever her personal beliefs may have been, her advocacy is an example of a truth we see often in Scripture:

> Learn to do what is good.
> Pursue justice.
> Correct the oppressor.
> Defend the rights of the fatherless.
> Plead the widow's cause.
>
> Isaiah 1:17

> This is what the LORD says: Administer justice and righteousness. Rescue the victim of robbery from his oppressor. Don't exploit or brutalize the resident alien, the fatherless, or the widow. Don't shed innocent blood in this place.
>
> Jeremiah 22:3

> The LORD of Armies says this: "Make fair decisions. Show faithful love and compassion to one another. Do not oppress the widow or the fatherless, the resident alien or the poor, and do not plot evil in your hearts against one another."
>
> Zechariah 7:9–10

We serve a God who advocates for the weak—for widows, for orphans, and for sojourners. We serve a God who condemns the manstealing that was the basis for slavery in the United States (Exodus 21:16). We serve a God who cares for those our culture routinely overlooks, unjustly rejects, or unfairly marginalizes.

Whatever Elizabeth's standing before our God, she understood at least part of his heart for his people on earth: that we would render true judgment, show kindness and mercy, and stand against oppression. Theodore Sedgwick, the man she worked for once she was free until the day she died—the man who helped her attain freedom—was said to be a Christian, and I hope that even though Elizabeth could not read the words of the Bible herself, she knew the God who made her for freedom, and that her earthly freedom pales in comparison to the freedom she knows with him in eternity.

Elizabeth and Me

I am still learning what it means to be a woman and an advocate.

Sometimes, it seems that our Christian ideals of femininity prize timidity over strength, placidity over courage, and docility over principle. But we have to remember that our culture has a way of shaping the Word of God to fit into our own ideals of what truly shapes a woman of God. Esther advocated for Israel with her husband, the king. Ruth advocated for herself with her future husband, Boaz. Deborah advocated for Israel as their judge.

And Elizabeth Freeman advocated for her freedom from the ungodly institution of American slavery and spent the rest of her life advocating for mothers who were bringing their babies into the world.

That part of the story is one of my favorites, because for me, advocacy looks like following in Elizabeth Freeman's footsteps in the birth field. It looks like learning all that I can about the history of gynecology and its adverse effects on Black women's bodies, as well as the modern-day attitudes and assumptions about Black health in general and Black maternal health specifically that lead to disparities in outcomes. It looks like knowing my rights when I enter a hospital and being able to advocate for my rights and the rights of my child. It means seeking as much education as I can to someday become a doula and advocate for the rights of other women.

Here's what I love: we don't all have to fight on the same front. We need midwives and doulas—we need educators, legislators, prison reformers, police reformers, wives, mothers, and sisters all on the front lines. As we strive to be faithful in whatever space the Lord has for us, *this* is the kind of strength that I love about Black women.

2

The Almost-
Forgotten Spitfire

Sara Griffith Stanley

Let scientific research produce elaborate expositions of the inferiority and mental idiosyncrasy of the colored race; one truth, the only essential truth, is incontrovertible:—The Omnipotent, Omniscient God's glorious autograph—the seal of angels—is written on our brows, that immortal characteristic of Divinity—the rational, mysterious and inexplicable soul, animates our frames.

—Sara Griffith Stanley

My parents almost named me Sarah.

They were so close, in fact, that my grandfather called to congratulate my dad on "Baby Sarah" when he heard I'd been born. All my life, I've laughed over the fact that I dodged one of the most common names for white women in the history of the world . . . only to be given a name that hovered in the top ten most popular names for Black baby girls throughout the nineties.

You probably know a Sarah. We *all* know a Sarah. And if not a Sarah, we know a Sarah Joy, a Sarah Elizabeth, a Sarah Anne, or a Sara. It is not a name that ever stood out to me before, unless I was teasing about the proliferation of Sarahs, Abigails, or Annas in any given homeschool group I attended growing up.

I often wonder why Sara G. Stanley's name stood out to me the very first time I read it. I had picked up the book *You Have Stept Out of Your Place: A History of Women and Religion in America* for another project I was working on. The name almost seemed a throwaway, listed alongside several other women (and more than one other Sarah) who were sent south as missionaries during the American Missionary Association's push to educate newly freed Black people in the South.

When I googled her name and hit images, I couldn't find a single picture of this woman. I found her Wikipedia page and read everything I could about her, though: abolitionist, teacher, writer, and missionary. My Wikipedia digging led me to an article called "Who Is Sufficient for These Things?" and I signed up for membership in a digital library (JSTOR) and paid $5 to download an eighteen-page article about Sara G. Stanley and the missionary association. At this point in my research, Sara wasn't going to be one of the main women profiled in this book, yet I had spent a good few hours combing through resources on a rabbit trail to find out all that I could about this woman.

The rabbit trail did not end there. One dissertation, a couple of academic articles, and a victorious purchase at AbeBooks later, and I held all of Sara Griffith Stanley's known letters in my hands. And I stood in my living room and I wept—not for the first time about this project, but definitely for the longest time—as a surge of awe overtook me.

Who is this woman who had me weeping to my husband that the mailman's delivery of *The Three Sarahs: Documents of Antebellum Black College Women* was the best thing that had ever happened to me? ("What about our marriage? Your children?" he asked. "Okay, *besides* that!" I responded through tears.)

I am so glad that you asked. And, honestly, more people should be asking.

A Fellow Teacher and Daughter of Teachers

Sara Griffith Stanley was born in New Bern, North Carolina, in 1837. Her grandfather, John C. Stanly (spelled without the *e*), was the illegitimate son of John Wright Stanly, a Georgia slave-owner.[1] When John W. Stanly died, Sara's grandfather inherited a great deal of wealth, as well as several slaves. He freed most of these enslaved people, and kept others, not as laborers on his land, but rather, in an effort "to permit them to remain in the town after the state legislature passed a law requiring that newly manumitted slaves must leave."[2]

Sara's father, John Stuart Stanley, founded and operated the Stanley School in New Bern, one of the few of its kind, which sought to educate free Black children in North Carolina. Sara's mother, Frances Griffith Stanley, taught at the school and raised and educated Sara and the five other Stanley children. The family were members of New Bern's Presbyterian church and had been since its founding. Every Sunday, Frances corralled her six children into the pews that John had purchased for them in the back of the white church. At this point in history, Black churches were illegal where Sara grew up.

Because of the ethnic heritage of John (and the similar ethnic heritage of Frances), the Stanleys were light-skinned Black Americans, "mulattoes," as they were called at the time, who could pass for white but chose not to. This is noteworthy, as many mulattoes of the Stanleys' time either chose to pass as white or to limit their interactions and society to similarly light-skinned Black people. The Stanleys, however, chose to make their heritage known and to associate with other Black families regardless of their skin tone. In her first letter to the American Missionary Association, Sara would write, "I am a colored woman; having a slight admixture of negro blood in my veins"[3] and later, "I am myself a colored woman, bound to that ignorant, degraded, and long-enslaved race, by ties of love and consanguinity; they are socially and politically 'my people.'"[4]

Sara would go on to be one of the very first college-educated Black women, graduating from Oberlin College and becoming, like her mother before her, a teacher. She would join the ranks of many prestigious Oberlin graduates—fellow Black women who flocked to the school to receive a rigorous education. Two years later, at the age of eighteen, she would reunite with her family as they fled the racism of the South to settle in Ohio.

Sara the Abolitionist

In addition to gracing her with her college education, giving her a start as a public school teacher, and being a place for reunion with her family, Ohio was also the place where Sara became an involved abolitionist.

In 1856, Sara wrote an address to the Ladies' Antislavery Society of Delaware, Ohio, of which she was a member, that so stirred her hearers it was read at the State Convention of Colored Men, which women were not allowed to speak at or attend.

It is in this speech—Sara's first published piece—that we are truly introduced to the spitfire from New Bern, North Carolina. She wrote,

> As the Alpine avalanche sweeps tumultously [sic] adown the mountain, overwhelming the peasant and his habitation, so

the conglomeration of hatred and prejudice against our race, brought together by perceptible accumulation, augmented and fostered by religion and science united, sweeps with seeming irresistible power toward us, menacing complete annihilation. But, should these things exercise a retarding influence upon our progressive efforts? Let American religion teach adoration to the demon Slavery, whom it denominates God: at the end, the book of record will show its falsity or truth. Let scientific research produce elaborate expositions of the inferiority and mental idiosyncrasy of the colored race; one truth, the only essential truth, is incontrovertible:—The Omnipotent, Omniscient God's glorious autograph—the seal of angels—is written on our brows, that immortal characteristic of Divinity—the rational, mysterious and inexplicable soul, animates our frames.[5]

Her words make me want to stand up and shout or sing a hallelujah chorus. Think about what she is saying here: let the Darwinism of the day make ludicrous arguments about the scientific inferiority of Black people—arguments used to defend and excuse the slave trade in all of its brutality—but history will show what we know to be true: that Black men and women are made in God's image.

This firm handle on theological truth was no accident: Sara's grandmother was one of the founding members of the New Bern Presbyterian church, and a quick perusal of Sara's letters shows that the family legacy included rigorous theological education. In fact, Sara described her parents as "pious and exemplary" in her religious education.[6] Throughout her letters, Sara expresses a deep understanding of the imago Dei—the understanding that man is created in the image of God. She goes so far as to talk about the image of God in the body of the Negro.

> Throughout her letters, Sara expresses a deep understanding of the imago Dei.

In her published speech, Sara lays into the hypocrisy of the American promise:

> These prerogatives American Republicanism, disregarding equity, humanity, and the fundamental principles of her national superstructure, has rendered a nonentity, while on her flag's transparencies and triumphal arches, stood beautifully those great, noble words: Liberty and Independence—Free Government—Church and State! And still they stand exponents of American character—her escutcheon wafts them on its star-spangled surface, to every clime—each ship load of emigrants from monarchical Europe, shout the words synonymous with Americans, their first paean in "the land of the free." . . . But strange incongruity! As the song of Freedom verberates and reverberates through the northern hills, and the lingering symphony quivers on the still air and then sinks away into silence, a low deep wail, heavy with anguish and despair, rises from the southern plains, and the clank of chains on human limbs mingles with the mournful cadence.[7]

Throughout her letters, Sara also displayed a profound understanding of civics. She understood her place as an American life. The promise of equality is one that many a Black American has had to clamor to hold America accountable for. Like Elizabeth Freeman before her, Sara staked her claim to that promise. And she enlarged on the legacy of Elizabeth Freeman by proclaiming that claim, not just for herself, but for every Black person in America.

Yet, unlike Elizabeth Freeman, Sara was blessed with a classical education and the ability to plead her cause, sharpening her pen into a well-aimed arrow of truth.

As a classically educated Black woman myself, I found her allusion to Greek literature especially beautiful:

> It was a Spartan mother's farewell to her son, "Bring home your shield or be brought upon it." To you we would say, be true,

be courageous, be steadfast in the discharge of your duty. The citadel of Error must yield to the unshrinking phalanx of truth. In our fireside circles, in the seclusion of our closets, we kneel in tearful supplication on your behalf.[8]

But though she was no stranger to pagan literature, it's the Word of God that permeated the end of her supplication. "As Christian wives, mothers and daughters, we invoke the blessing of the King, Eternal and Immortal, 'who sitteth upon the circle of the earth, who made the heavens with all their host,' to rest upon you . . ."[9]

Little is known about Sara's life between this speech and the ensuing Civil War. She taught in the Ohio public school system on and off, dividing her time between her young charges and her family. But when the Civil War ended, she saw a need, and, as she instructed in her dynamic speech, she rose to fill it.

The Spitfire Arrives

The American Missionary Association was a Protestant abolitionist group that devoted itself to the religious education of freed people. They played an integral part in the founding of several historically Black colleges that survive to this day: Fisk, Howard, Tugaloo (here in Mississippi), and others. They also sent many northern teachers—both Black and white—to the South in the wake of the Civil War to teach the newly emancipated.

It was to this mission that Sara was drawn in 1864. At the age of twenty-five, she wrote her very first letter to the American Missionary Association, requesting a position as a teacher in their ranks. She wrote,

"This is the way, walk ye in it," speaks a voice within my heart, and I know that no thought of suffering and privation, nor even death, should deter me from making every effort possible for the moral and intellectual salvation of these ignorant and degraded people; children of a beneficent father, and heirs of the kingdom of Heaven. And I feel moreover how much greater my own spiritual advancement will be, for while laboring for them, while living a life of daily toil, self sacrifice, and denial, I can dwell nearer to God and my Savior and become constantly, by divine aid, richer in faith, richer in love, richer in all the graces of the Holy Spirit.[10]

Sara was first sent to Norfolk, Virginia, with an integrated teaching unit. There she began the work of educating newly freed children. Sara would travel to several cities as a teacher for the AMA, but it was in Virginia where her reputation hit a snag. Unaccustomed to a Black woman who saw herself as completely the equal of every white teacher she encountered, both Black and white teachers bristled at Sara's attitude.

Sara herself found much to bristle about. Her biggest complaint about her station in Virginia was the racism of the fellow teachers. After witnessing an incident of racism, Sara (of course) did not hold her tongue. She wrote to the powers that be protesting the offender and making the case that he did "great harm" to the cause the AMA claimed to stand for. Her letter held all of her characteristically pointed verbiage, her tightly controlled passion, and her passion for the truth of the Gospel:

As I have understood the religion of Christ, the brotherhood of man is its fundamental and elementary constituent—"Whatsoever ye would"—"God has created of *one* blood"— "Let us love one another. He that loveth not knoweth not God, for God is love."—"He that loveth not his brother whom he hath seen, how can he love God whom he hath not seen?" etc., etc. The propagandist then of a religion which denies the *first* principle of the Gospel, viz. "The Fatherhood of God and the Brotherhood of Christ," not only disseminating his views to those who legitimately belong to his own household, but promoting the moral, mental and spiritual welfare of the Freed people, is irrefragably laboring for the advancement of the kingdom of Satan. As that martyr saint of Harper's Ferry remarked of a Southern clergyman who visited him while imprisoned "He needs to learn the ABC of Christianity."[11]

A Love Letter to Sara G. Stanley

These were the very first words I ever read by Sara Griffith Stanley—that a racist teacher was, through his racism, "laboring for the advancement of the kingdom of Satan" and that he needed to go back and "learn the ABC of Christianity." With those two phrases, she captured my heart like no other figure in this book has done, incredible women though they are.

In Sara, I see whispers of myself: born to privilege, given every educational advantage her parents could afford her, raised with a rigorous religious education, raised in the church, working as a teacher, living at home until her mid-twenties. . . . I'm likely the descendant of a slaveowner, with a lighter-skinned family tree that barely looks related to my unambiguous brown skin.

There is just enough in Sara's story to strike a familiar chord in me.

And just enough in Sara's story to inspire awe about the dynamo that this woman truly was. She traded a privileged northern existence to walk into the minefield of the reconstructed South. She stood toe-to-toe with racists in the midst of teachers who were supposedly there to *help* the newly freed Black people they taught. In a time when some teachers wrote more favorably about lighter-skinned students than darker-skinned ones, when some teachers refused to board with their Black co-laborers, Sara spoke up.

Not only did she speak up—she spoke up as a *Black* woman. In spite of the fact that she could have passed for a white woman—no doubt garnering more safety, more freedom, less suspicion, less judgment—she chose to fully acknowledge the heritage God had given her. And not only did Sara acknowledge it, she was proud of it.

I stood in my living room crying with her letters in my hands because Sara Griffith Stanley offered me at thirty what I wish I had had at ten, twelve, or fourteen, growing up in my predominately white surroundings: the gumption to be vocally Christian, vocally Black, and vocally proud of the identity that the Lord had chosen for me. The ability not to be afraid of being the most intelligent woman in the room—the most outspoken woman in the room—the only Black woman in the room.

The hue of my skin and the hue of Sara Stanley's skin could not be more different, but the similarity of our heritage was something she never denied.

Let that sink in. Sara was born in the 1830s. Slavery was still rampant across the American South, but her family lived as freedmen in North Carolina. Rather than blend into New Bern white society, her father founded a school specifically for the education of Black children. Her mother associated with Black women who were far from ethnically ambiguous. Sara herself attended one of the few colleges of the time that admitted Black women and owned her heritage proudly. Not only that, but she fought on behalf of those less privileged than she.

And not only *that*, but she went *to the South* in the wake of the Civil War and dared hold her head high as a woman of color in racism's midst.

How could one *not* be in love with the story of this dynamic woman? How could one not stop to meditate on how much her decisions cost her?

How have we forgotten her name?

The End of Sara's Story

Sara worked for the American Missionary Association for a number of years. She went on to marry a white man (causing a bit of a stir) and left the AMA shortly after. The details of her life are spotty after that. Now Sara Woodward, she lost a child in infancy and became a widow. She spent some time at Lucy Craft Laney's school in Georgia, aiding another dynamic woman in her life's mission to educate the Black masses. (Laney's story is another that I will tell.)

And yet, "at the time of her death in 1918, at the age of 82, she was receiving a government pension of $25."[12] The place of her death and burial is unknown, and to historians' knowledge, she left behind no family to call her own.

The end of her story weighs heavy on my heart—as well as the fact that so few have known her story. Had I not run across her name in a random line of text and typed it into Google, I would not know her story myself to tell it to you.

> To tell the stories of Black women in history, we must become dogged researchers.

More than any other figure in these pages (closely followed by Maria Fearing, of whom we at least have pictures), Sara Griffith Stanley Woodward taught me that in order to tell the stories of so many Black women in history, we must become dogged researchers. We must comb footnotes, obtain rare books, speak to the experts, and above all, pray for favor from the storytelling God we serve.

As historian Daina Ramey Berry notes,

We pay homage to and draw on an abundant historiography about Black women, in addition to scouring archives for precious primary source material. Whenever possible, we also make use of the growing repositories of historical and archival records online, and we often quote documentary interviews and cite video footage featuring Black women. Our hope is that this approach will more easily assist any readers who want to find out more about many of the figures and subjects in the book. Even with these efforts, there are times the historical record fails to adequately document Black women's experiences. Sometimes there are hardly any records at all. As historians we often find ourselves in the difficult position of relying on archival records not penned by Black women but instead chronicled by those who played central roles in obscuring and silencing their legacies.[13]

This is the fate of many a historical woman, but it is especially true of Black American women, particularly for laypeople searching out their stories. Without access to an academic library, I couldn't secure photocopies of Oberlin historians' extensive research on these women. Because of COVID-19, the American Missionary Association's archives weren't as accessible as they normally are.

And as a layperson, not an academic, I wouldn't have even known to lament the lack of primary sources if one name in one paragraph of one obscure book hadn't mentioned Sara Griffith Stanley's name. I wouldn't have even known there was "enough" information to write about her if my friend Abena Wright hadn't used her extensive knowledge as a PhD candidate to point me down the right paths and encourage me to keep digging.

Sara was the first woman to send me burrowing down the rabbit hole of research, scouring for clues, digging for treasure until I struck the gold of her actual letters: a living testament to the fact that she existed. And not only did she exist, but hundreds of thousands of faceless, nameless women exist, with stories worth knowing—with stories worth telling. I wish I could tell them all, but for now, I've narrowed it to the ten who clung to me long after I closed the book on their words.

The Beginning of Our Story

The ending of Sara Griffith Stanley's story is still at the beginning of ours. This woman's voice roared out of the silence of the historical account, and I heard her, loud and clear. And now, you get to hear her—to learn from her.

You get to learn that shining example of educated Black womanhood, and you get to teach her story to as many others as you choose. You get to carry on her legacy with rigorous education, undaunted Christian conviction, and the unapologetic defense and protection of the marginalized.

Sara was not perfect. There are places in her letters that still hold some of the prejudice of the day. There is an unspecified incident that resulted in her being disciplined by the AMA and repenting of wrongdoing. The reports of her haughty attitude may not have been driven merely by jealousy or misunderstandings. The woman was flawed in ways that we might be able to read between the lines—and in ways that we never will.

And yet, those flaws do not keep hers from being a story I am so grateful that I get to tell. If I could bottle up the feeling of finally reading her letters after months of digging, searching, and praying, I would have a scratch-and-sniff sticker on this page! But hopefully my words have conveyed just a hint of the privilege it is to know her story.

She died in obscurity. But she did not die without a legacy. Even my telling of her story on these pages is part of that legacy—your reading her story is part of that legacy. The lives of all of the educated Black women who came after her are part of her legacy.

Even mine.

When I was a young girl, I remember telling my mom that I just wanted to be *remembered*. The William Shakespeare, not the Billy Spears who wrote really excellent community theater plays and died in obscurity. The older I've gotten, though, the more I've realized that fame is not the only measure of our impact.

The average person on the street has no idea who Sara G. Stanley was. And yet, her impact changed the lives of the students she came in contact with. Hundreds of years later, it changed *my* life. Her faithfulness, so broadly unseen, resonates with this girl who used to want *all the credit*. Her impact was not broad—but it was deep. And that's the kind of impact I want.

The Instagram followers, Twitter count, Facebook likes . . . those are not nearly as important as the lives I'm touching day-to-day: for me, my children. For Sara, her students. *That's* the true test of faithfulness.

I had this legacy in mind as I sat in the passenger seat on a road trip with my husband the other day. We were daydreaming about the future, and I said, "I think I really like the name Sara."

"*Sara?*" He was shocked, both because I've told him my almost-Sarah story, and because I'm a committed boy mom. But we love to name our children after the people who inspire us.

And with inspiration as the litmus test, Sara is one of the most beautiful names I've ever heard.

3

The One I Almost Left Out
Nannie Helen Burroughs

The honor of black womanhood is at stake, and let those who will, cower before the crisis, but let us here, in this place, put ourselves on record as protectors and defenders of Christian womanhood, white or black.

—Nannie Helen Burroughs

As was the case with almost every other woman in this book, I had not heard of Nannie Helen Burroughs until I began working on this project. I was in the process of whittling down the number of women I wanted to profile from about twenty to ten, and was at that place where things start to feel a little arbitrary: I feel *slightly* more connected to this woman than that one . . . this one has a body of work that I like a *little* more . . . this one is someone people might have already read about elsewhere, even if I haven't read about her extensively yet. . . .

And Nannie almost bit the dust, because although my initial reaction to her was jumping-up-and-down excitement, I ended up picking up a book called *Twelve Things the Negro Must Do* that just about put her on the chopping block.

The book itself is a collection of essays about a shorter essay Nannie wrote. In it, she sets her sights on improving the "Negro race" through such advice as "he is entirely too loud and too ill-mannered"[1] and too apt to blame white people for his failures. The commentary I read painted Nannie as a prophet to the ills of Black American living, and I'll admit: I cringed.

Growing up as the only Black woman in many a predominately white surrounding, I have grown wary of the idea that respectability is the answer to racism. Booker T. Washington (to whom Nannie was often likened as his female counterpart) famously advocated that the best way for Black people to overcome prejudice in society was to *earn* their place by being economically independent, financially responsible, and socially acceptable. It sounds logical enough on its face: what better way to uplift the ethnicity than to *prove* our worth through hard work and industry?

As a Black woman who grew up with two incredibly respectable parents in upper-middle-class surroundings, I am bound to report: respectability is not the answer to prejudice. If I had a quarter for every "pretty for a black girl," "smart for a black girl," "articulate for a black girl," "well-mannered for a black girl" comment I received growing up . . . well, I'd be even wealthier and therefore, even *more* respectable by some of black history's standards. I've never been guilty of any of the twelve things Nannie states that Negroes must not do—by sheer nature of the fact that I was born to privilege—and yet I've still been the target of overt (and underhanded) racism.

Respect shouldn't be something that has to be earned. Sara G. Stanley has already given us the words here: we are made in God's image—*God's image in the body of a Negro*—and that is why we merit respect and honor. Not because of anything that we bring to the table.

If Nannie Helen Burroughs was going to "fix her mouth" (in the words of my southern mother) to say that all Black people have to do to gain respect is to *be* respect-worthy, I wasn't here for it. I did not want to include a woman in my book who reinforced the fallacious idea that prejudice is a byproduct of Black failing.

Instead, I found a woman who once said "the law ignores the fact that beneath the black skin is a soul as immortal, a pride as exalted, an intellect as keen, a longing as intense and aspirations as noble, as those which peep forth and manifest themselves in the proudest blue-eyed Anglo-Saxon man or woman."[2]

A woman who told white people to "STOP putting all kinds of barriers in the way of the progress of the Negro race, and then declaring that America's high purpose is to build 'one nation indivisible, with LIBERTY and JUSTICE for ALL'" and to "STOP using Negroes as political mud sills and stepping stones, to get whites in power, politically, and then deny Negroes full citizenship rights and equal opportunities" (her emphasis).[3]

A woman who said,

Every human being is made in the image of God. A human soul spells divinity and eternity. Touch it and you touch God. The majority of white people have little or no respect for personality unless that personality is clothed in white skin. The survival of this civilization depends absolutely upon whether the white race can be cured of its un-Godly white complex. There can be no compromise, or physical arrangement in race relations that will give lasting peace, unless the white race decides to make intensive teaching of reverence for human personality, the fundamental thing in race relations. This is the price of Democracy on this planet.[4]

That woman is still, in fact, Nannie Helen Burroughs. The same woman who argued that "In any race, only those are inferior who do inferior things."[5]

You see, the more I read about Nannie, the more I realized that she wasn't a one-sided political pundit or a token—that in fact, she railed against one-sidedness and tokenism. She was, instead, a thorough and consistent cultural commentator who cared enough about her Black Christian brethren to preach for their improvement, and who cared enough about her white Christian brethren to hold them accountable in those areas where improvement was limited due to ethnicity.

In a world rife with tribalism, unapologetically one-sided rhetoric, and willing political pawns, Nannie Helen Burroughs surprised me. I think she'll surprise you, too.

The Genesis of Nannie

Nannie Helen Burroughs was born in 1879 in Orange, Virginia, the older of two daughters. Nannie's younger sister and father would die during her early childhood. Her mother, Jennie—a formerly enslaved woman—would move with Nannie to find a better life in Washington, DC, in 1883.

Nannie and Jennie would live in relative poverty in the nation's capital. Decades later, activist Malcolm X would describe the squalor of his WWII-era DC travels this way:

> Then, on the overnight layover, I naturally went sightseeing in downtown Washington. I was astounded to find in the nation's capital, just a few blocks from Capitol Hill, thousands of Negroes living worse than any I'd ever seen in the poorest sections of Roxbury; in dirt-floor shacks along unspeakably

filthy lanes with names like Pig Alley and Goat Alley. I had seen a lot, but never such a dense concentration of stumblebums, pushers, hookers, public crap-shooters, even little kids running around at midnight begging for pennies, half-naked and barefooted. Some of the railroad cooks and waiters had told me to be very careful, because muggings, knifings and robberies went on every night among these Negroes . . . just a few blocks from the White House.

But I saw other Negroes better off; they lived in blocks of rundown red brick houses. The old "Colonial" railroaders had told me about Washington having a lot of "middle-class" Negroes with Howard University degrees, who were working as laborers, janitors, porters, guards, taxi-drivers, and the like. For the Negro in Washington, mail-carrying was a prestige job.[6]

Though Nannie was raised in poverty, she was afforded every educational opportunity Jennie could provide. The girl would graduate from the famous M Street High School, a prestigious educational facility run by graduates of Sara G. Stanley's alma mater, Oberlin College. Mary Church Terrell—one of the founders of the National Association of Colored Women and the first Black woman to serve on the DC Board of Education—was one of Nannie's teachers, as was Mary Jane Patterson, the first Black woman in the United States to graduate from college with a bachelor's degree.

"In any race, only those are inferior who do inferior things."

Ever the go-getter, Nannie would graduate M Street with honors in 1896, founding the Harriet Beecher Stowe Literary Society during her tenure as a student.[7] However, though more than qualified to teach, she would be denied a position in the DC school system, later citing colorism as the likely reason. Most of the highly favored and sought-after teachers of the period were several shades lighter than caramel-colored

Nannie, the Black aristocracy in DC being made up largely of light-skinned Black folks with strong connections.

Never one to let prejudice deter her, Nannie forged her own path, working as a janitor before moving to Philadelphia and becoming bookkeeper and stenographer for the Foreign Mission Board of the National Baptist Convention.

In the evenings, Nannie taught typing, shorthand, and book-keeping classes, as well as courses in domestic arts—millinery, sewing, cooking—to help women become more efficient in household management. For members of the women's industrial club, the classes cost ten cents per week. As the classes grew in popularity, Nannie received financial backing to hire more teachers. This freed her to supervise and further develop the evening school.[8]

This evening school would be the precursor for much of Nannie's work in the education of young Black women, but before that, she would also start a successful side business, the Negro Picture Calendar, which was a "precursor for Ebony magazine."[9]

In 1900, Nannie would give the speech that launched her into the national spotlight, "How the Sisters Are Hindered from Helping" at the National Baptist Convention. Arguing for the inclusion of women and their perspective in missions both local and abroad, Nannie said,

> We come now to the rescue. We unfurl our banner upon which is inscribed this motto, "The World for Christ. Woman, Arise, He calleth for Thee." Will you as a pastor and friend of missions help by not hindering these women when they come among you to speak and to enlist the women of your church? It has ever been from the time of Miriam, that most remarkable woman, the sister of Moses, that most remarkable man, down to the courageous women that in very recent years have carried the Gospel into Tibet and Africa and proclaimed and taught the

truth where no man has been allowed to enter. Surely, women somehow have had a very important part in the work of saving this redeemed earth.[10]

She would spend the rest of her life as one of those very helpful sisters, founding the Women's Industrial Club of Kentucky, opening the National Training School for Women, founding the National Association of Wage Earners, helping to organize the International Council of Women of the Darker Races, and serving as president of the Women's Convention at the National Baptist Convention and on the executive committee of the Baptist World Alliance. She would also spend her entire life writing: as a recurring columnist for *The Courier*, editor of *The Worker* magazine, oft keynote speaker, and the recipient of an honorary master's degree from Eckstein-Norton University in Kentucky. She would work tirelessly until her death in 1961.

Radical Consistency

Nannie Helen Burroughs's accomplishments are staggering by any estimation. The woman never stopped. She wrote that work was "the only way any people can succeed,"[11] and she lived by her mantra. She worked tirelessly, wrote endlessly, and spoke fearlessly.

And yet, before I began this project, I did not know who she was. Unlike Sara G. Stanley, Nannie is shown in numerous pictures—as a beautiful, smiling woman, coarse hair piled on top of her head, always clad in the fashion of the day. She has a body of work more prolific than any other woman in these pages. During her lifetime, she was known as the "female Booker T. Washington."

One of my main resources in learning more about Nannie are her own words, captured in *Nannie Helen Burroughs: A Documentary Portrait of an Early Civil Rights Pioneer, 1900–1959*.

The book includes more than fifty essays by the activist, ranging from the theological to the social, from scathing critiques of the Black community's downfalls to unflinching criticisms of white American racism, from boldly uplifting women's voices and contributions to chastising them for neglecting the haven of their home, from supporting men in the battle to telling men to *get out of her way.*

And perhaps that is why Nannie's legacy has been obscured in the twenty-first century: she is hard to pigeonhole.

I myself tried to pigeonhole her when I first read her work— I found myself likening her to a certain modern-day political pundit who makes her living by critiquing the Black community for a majority-white audience—with very little positive public interaction with the Black community.

But I was foolish.

One of the most amazing facets about Nannie Helen Burroughs is that for all of her critiques of the Black community— and there were many—she spent her life pouring into that community. Nannie wasn't talking for shock value, or to impress white people with her comparative Black consciousness. She was speaking out of a real and demonstrated care for the Black community. They were her priority, always. She put her money where her mouth was, over and over again, until the day she died. *She was not just a woman of words, but a woman of action.*

She once said,

What's the sense of talk if you don't do something? You talk and people get stirred up and think they'd like to do something, and that makes them feel good; and they go off happy and satisfied, feeling as though they're some account in the world because they've felt like doing something and they haven't done one thing to help one soul alive. If you're going to be a Christian you've got to do something weekdays as well as talk and feel about it on Sundays.[12]

And Nannie left a legacy of *doing*.

One of the reasons the pundits of today fail to stir us is because they are more prone to talking than doing. They grandstand, idealogues who are more adept at turning a phrase than applying their hands to the hard work. This is nothing new—it's something that Nannie noticed even in her day, and abhorred.

As much as Nannie's unwavering criticism of Black Americans may seem unhelpful to a modern-day reader, she *cared* about the people she critiqued. She truly believed in the fruit of the advancement of her kinspeople, and she spent her life working toward it.

A Faithful Platform

I am a millennial. I feel no shame in that declaration—I was born in 1990, and it is what it is. But part of belonging to that oft-critiqued generation is that I am uniquely aware of my platform and have been since early adulthood.

No longer does one need to be the founder of several prestigious organizations, a proven author and thinker, or a professional to have a say in everyday discourse. We have arrived at a moment in history when every person in America is allowed to have a voice—as long as he has internet access. Our Facebook pages, Twitter feeds, curated Instagram videos, and whatever new social platform will be trending by the time these words are published give us a sense of authority before we've even been tested.

If you're anything like I am, it can often feel threatening. I open my Twitter with fear and trembling, debating over the wording of every mundane update, trying to make sure that nothing I'm going to say will offend the wrong people, trying to make sure that everything I *want* to say reaches the ears of the right people. And care is good—God's Word talks about having care in our speech.

But so often, that care is more about man's glory than God's. It's about curating an image. I want to be seen a certain way—I want to be *branded* a certain way. Often, that "brand" has kept me from speaking out on certain issues, using certain verbiage, or confronting certain people. I have a box and I'm comfortable in it.

Nannie's words don't always fit in my box.

Nannie's words don't always fit into *anyone's* box.

Least of all the 280-character Twitter box that so often defines me.

Take, for instance, her response to Billy Sunday—the most popular evangelist of his era—when he proposed teaching a segregated revival service. Where I might have written a subtweet about how I would not attend a segregated service, Nannie addressed Billy Sunday directly:

> You must be under the impression that the Colored people of this city want to hear you. This is not true. However . . . they may be willing to arrange for a "performance" at one of their own churches . . . If the weather is favorable, but we cannot promise, even under favorable weather conditions . . . to have any intelligent Negroes see and hear you. Those who might attend would be just as ignorant as the Negroes in Atlanta who accommodated you.[13]

Do we all need to approach conflict the exact same way as Nannie Helen Burroughs? I hope not. Because, personality-wise, I could not be *less* like this woman. And like Sara Stanley and Elizabeth Freeman before her, she was not perfect—as no Christian hero is.

However, that does not mean I don't have much to learn from Nannie's legacy. She was not just an empty talker, but was, rather, a *doer*. And that is a litmus test for hypocrisy if I've ever heard of one.

As easy as it is to rattle off a tweet about my opinion . . . am I putting my money where my mouth is? If I critique something, am I working to fix it? If I critique someone, am I invested in their growth? If I point out a problem, am I willing to invest time and energy to repair it?

Because Nannie was.

She did not sit far off and lambast the Black community for not meeting her standards—she got elbow deep in the community and discipled countless young women. She did not nitpick the government as an uninvolved citizen—she rolled up her sleeves and got to work to steer her country.

She talked a *lot*. But she acted even more. And image consciousness was not one of her personality traits. In fact, her biggest worry in life was that she wasn't doing *enough*.

Nannie's Legacy

The book that first sparked my intense excitement for research about these women was *Women Builders* by Sadie Iola Daniel. I found the title in a photocopied church newsletter on JSTOR and hunted down the only copy on Amazon—an out-of-print second edition. In 1931, Daniel profiled women like Lucy Craft Laney, Maggie Lena Walker, Janie Porter Barrett, and Nannie Helen Burroughs.

> Nannie talked a **lot**. But she acted even more.

I picked up the book without a single thought to Nannie, little knowing how important this woman would become to me. It has now become one of my most prized resources, in large part *because* it profiles this unstoppable woman.

And yet, Nannie questioned that she should be included in the volume at all:

In a letter to her friend Carter G. Woodson, Burroughs bemoaned a chapter about her in Sadie Daniel's *Women Builders* (1931) as premature: "I have not done enough to be given a place in any book I hope to accomplish something that will be enduring and really constructive, but up to now I am woefully disgusted with what I have been able to accomplish for the women and girls of my race." By the time of the letter's writing, Nannie Helen Burroughs had founded the National Training School for Women and Girls, of which she had been principal for over twenty years, had established several successful women's organizations, and was a prominent member of nearly a dozen others. She had also been appointed by President Herbert Hoover to chair a fact-finding committee on Negro housing. Yet she was thoroughly underwhelmed with her accomplishments.[14]

She never sat down to rest. Not until the day she died. Eschewing marriage and motherhood, both of which she prized highly, she devoted her life to her cause.

Again, one does not have to serve the exact same way Nannie did to be an asset to the kingdom of Christ. But we do have to understand what Nannie understood. Of the Bible, she said,

Man's highest faculties and noblest views are developed and refined by its benign light of revelation. It makes of each human being a flower in the garden of humanity. It drops into each soul the dew of heaven—sympathy, kindness, love, so that when that soul is shaken (moved) by the wind, it lets fall some dew drops to the roots of others in the garden of humanity and each soul thereby, becomes a nourisher of others.[15]

And in typical Nannie fashion, she had this critique to level at the churches of her day:

The missionary fires in most of our churches burn very low, because an overwhelming majority of our church members know something "ABOUT" Jesus Christ, but do not know Jesus Christ. We have our lamps, but we have no oil; if we have oil our lamps are not trimmed; if they are trimmed they are not burning; if they are burning they are under a bushel. If you are looking for foolish virgins don't look in the Bible, look in our churches. The world needs light. It is walking in darkness because the church is filled with foolish virgins. The leadership is not spiritually wise. God does not call the blind to lead the blind—nor cowards to preach His gospel.[16]

She wrote these words seventy years ago—in an era that many evangelicals consider to be a spiritual heyday for American culture. And yet, they still ring true for us today, don't they? We are meant to be a light to the nations, but we walk in the darkness of hypocrisy.

Once more, we do not have to live our lives the way that Nannie did. One of the things I hope this book illustrates is that even though all of these women were teachers, they taught in very different ways. But the current that flows through Nannie's life is the same current that flows throughout the lives of the rest of these women—the same current that should flow through our lives: the Gospel of Christ. While we may not serve exactly as Nannie did, we *must* have the same motivator for our service—and, yes, the Sunday school answer holds true here: it's Jesus.

Loving through Differences

Nannie's words never fail to challenge me. Sometimes, they challenge my long-held assumptions; sometimes, they challenge my inactivity; sometimes, they challenge my laziness; sometimes, they challenge me to speak up; and sometimes, they just challenge my patience, because I disagree with the way she says certain things.

But I cannot disagree with this woman's work ethic. And I cannot disagree that the fact that hers is a name I never knew is one of the tragedies I am most excited to right for others in these pages.

Black women are not a monolith. *Of course not,* comes my immediate agreement to that statement. But if that is true, then Nannie should be embraced as a sister, not side-eyed as too much of a challenge. It is completely possible to disagree with some of her thoughts about respectability while lauding her consistency, her work ethic, and her devotion to Christ and his people.

Nannie died at the age of eighty-two. At this writing, I have just entered my thirties. She lived and thrived in a historical moment that I cannot imagine. And she spent many days of her life paving the way for me to be able to grow up in a world where I have a voice—even if it dissents from hers in some ways. For that, I am forever grateful.

Nannie once said,

The Negro woman "totes" more water; hoes more corn; picks more cotton; washes more clothes; cooks more meals; nurses more babies; mammies more Nordics; supports more churches; does more race uplifting; serves as mud-sills for more climbers; takes more punishment; does more forgiving; gets less protection and appreciation, than do the women in any other civilized group in the world.[17]

Nannie entered into glory a shining example of this very sentiment. She did it all, paving the way for us to do our part behind her. It is a privilege to stand in her shadow.

Inspired by the Bronze Muse

Frances Ellen Watkins Harper

The robes of womanhood that were of this world were fickle yet indispensable tools in the battle for racial uplift, but mere trifles compared to the garments of glory that some women glimpsed or felt in visions, and others looked forward to in "the holy companionship of heaven."

—Frances Ellen Watkins Harper

I was eight years old when I wrote my first "novel."

It was an uplifting tale that ended in the death of every single character—including the narrator. If memory serves, the very last words were, "I lay down in the snow and die."

To my mother's credit, rather than thinking she had a sociopath on her hands, she encouraged my vivid imagination. When my dad would go out of town, I would climb into bed with her and read aloud from my latest "novels" until we fell asleep. She showed a keen interest in every character I spun and put as many books in front of me as she could. My writing voice was shaped by Jane Austen's *Emma*, Emily Brontë's *Wuthering Heights*, Lucy Maud Montgomery's *Anne of Green Gables*, Louisa May Alcott's *Little Women*, and Harper Lee's *To Kill a Mockingbird*.

I only remember one Black novelist from my childhood: Mildred D. Taylor. When I found her, I set out to devour every word she'd written. Her novels and her short stories were probably the most influential puzzle pieces of my childhood writing journey. Unlike the other books I devoured (and really, truly loved), Mildred's gave me Cassie Logan, a main character who looked like me. But as influential as Cassie Logan's existence was, the most mind-boggling element of the *Roll of Thunder* canon wasn't the main character but, rather, the author herself. Mildred DeLois Taylor, born in 1943 in Jackson, Mississippi, spun tales close to my own southern heart and home.

And maybe I could be a storyteller someday, too.

Imagine my surprise as a thirty-year-old when I realized that I had never heard of one of Mildred's forebearers—the first Black woman in the United States to publish a short story. Imagine my shock at realizing that she not only penned short stories—but also poetry, novels, and speeches.

Imagine what ten-year-old Jasmine would have felt knowing that at the end of the nineteenth century, Frances Ellen Watkins Harper was one of the most renowned public figures of the Black community, only to realize here, at the beginning of the twenty-first, that little Black girls all over America did not even know her name.

Frances's Story

Frances Ellen Watkins was born on September 24, 1825, in Baltimore, Maryland. Her parents were both free but died before young Frances reached the age of three. Her uncle, Reverend William Watkins, became her guardian. Frances was educated at her uncle's school, the William Watkins Academy for Colored Youth.[1] It was under her uncle's tutelage that Frances developed the strong Christian convictions that would resonate in her writing throughout her lifetime.

Frances left school at the age of fourteen to support herself. Unafraid of hard work, she took on several jobs, including teaching. At twenty-eight, though, she found her life's calling: Frances would be a lecturer on the anti-slavery circuit, applying her sterling rhetoric to the cause of freedom.

Wrote one historian,

> In addition to her lecturing and writing, Harper was a social activist on quite equal footing with any white, middle-class woman of her time. She was a member of the American Women's Suffrage Association, the Women's Christian Temperance Union, the American Equal Rights Association, the National Council of Negro Women, the American Association for the Education of Colored Youth, the Universal Peace Union, and the John Brown Memorial Association of Women.[2]

Said another, "Her countless public speeches throughout the second half of the nineteenth century mesmerized audiences from Mississippi to Maine."[3]

Frances would continue to cultivate her talent as a poet and author as well, publishing a collection of poems called *Forest Leaves, also called Autumn Leaves,* in 1854 and her short story "The Two Offers" in 1859, and releasing several other poetry collections and short stories. She incorporated her poetry in the stirring prose of her speeches often. Some of her favorite lines were from her poem "Bury Me in a Free Land" which says, "Make me a grave where'er you will; / In a lowly plain or a lofty hill; / Make it among earth's humblest graves; / But not in a land where men are slaves"[4] Her two examples in the abolitionist cause were her uncle, who was a devout abolitionist his entire life, and her friend William Sill, called the Father of the Underground Railroad because of the work he did ushering more than eight hundred refugees to freedom.[5]

Frances's speeches stood up even to the scrutiny of Confederate journalists:

> Her voice was remarkable—as sweet as any woman's voice we have ever heard, and so clear and distinct as to pass every syllable to the most distant ear in the house. . . . We followed the speaker to the end, not discerning a single grammatical inaccuracy of speech, or the slightest violation of good taste. At times the current of thoughts flowed in eloquent and poetic expression. . . . The main theme of her discourse was the grand opportunity that emancipation had afforded the black race.[6]

Indeed, the same dynamic force employed in her poetry was stirringly employed in her rhetoric, to such a degree that some white listeners speculated that she couldn't possibly be a Black woman. Wrote Frances to a friend:

> I don't know but that you would laugh if you were to hear some of the remarks which my lectures call forth: "She is a man," again "She is not colored, she is painted." . . . Both white and colored come out to hear me, and I have very fine meetings. . . . I am standing with my race on the threshold of a new era, and though some be far past me in the learning of the schools, yet to-day, with my limited fragmentary knowledge, I may help the race forward a little.[7]

Her poise, rhetorical skill, and passion earned her the nickname The Bronze Muse, a title that pointed to the fact that Frances was a master of the English language in speech, poetry, and prose. She realized that she was an ambassador for her entire ethnicity every time she mounted the stage, and she did her people proud, her own ability for intelligent and articulate arguments proof of her claims of equality.

What I love about Frances is how thoroughly her poetic ability seeped into her rhetorical moments. She was every bit a poet in the lectern and every bit a principled orator in her poetry. Frances had a knack for uniting all parts of her skill in service for her cause.

> Frances had a knack for uniting all parts of her skill in service for her cause.

It is said that the negro is ignorant. But why is he ignorant? It comes with ill grace from a man who has put out my eyes to make a parade of my blindness—to reproach my poverty when he has wronged me of my money. If the negro is ignorant, he has lived under the shadow of an institution which, at least in part of the country, made it a crime to teach him to read the name of the ever-blessed Christ. If he is poor, what has become of the money he has been earning for the last two hundred and fifty years? Years ago it was said cotton fights and cotton conquers for American slavery. The negro helped build up the great cotton power of the South, and in the North his sigh was heard in the whir of its machinery, and his blood and tears upon the warp and woof of its manufacturers.[8]

Like many of the staunchest abolitionists of her day, Frances extended her advocacy to American women as well as enslaved Black Americans.

If the fifteenth century discovered America to the Old World, the nineteenth century is discovering woman to herself. Little did Columbus imagine when the New World broke upon his vision like a lovely gem in the coronet of the universe, the glorious

71

possibilities of a land where the sun should be our engraver, the winged lightning our messenger, and steam our beast of burden. But as mind is more than matter, and the highest ideal always the true real, so to women comes the opportunity to strive for richer and grander discoveries than ever gladdened the eye of the Genoese mariner.

Not the opportunity of discovering new worlds, but that of filling this old world with fairer and higher aims than the greed of gold and lust of power, is hers. Through weary, wasting years men have destroyed, dashed in pieces, and overthrown, but today we stand on the threshold of women's era, and woman's work is grandly constructive. In her hand are possibilities whose use or abuse must tell upon the political life of the nation, and send their influence for good or evil across the track of unborn ages.[9]

No one exemplified the true force of these words more handily than Frances Ellen Watkins Harper. She viewed her femininity not as a liability to the causes she championed but as an asset. Journalist Sarah Greenwood would describe Frances this way:

> She stands quietly beside her desk, and speaks without notes, with gestures few and fitting. Her manner is marked by dignity and composure. She is never assuming, never theatrical. . . . The woe of two hundred years sighed through her tones. Every glance of her sad eyes was a mournful remonstrance against injustice and wrong.[10]

In a time when many women would settle down and evade the spotlight once married, Frances prioritized her work throughout her life. A common trend with the women I've chosen to profile in this book is their commitment to a cause outside of marriage. Many of them were widows, some never married, some were mothers of children who died in infancy, others raised only one child. This selection process was not by design, but in a Christian subculture that tends to prize marriage and children as *the* foremost ways of bringing glory to God and pursuing Christian service as a woman, these ten women were able to have fruitful lives of active service for God's glory without settling down.

I am no less committed to my husband and two children for my admiration of Frances, but I am encouraged that the body of Christ works in diverse ways to accomplish his glorious purposes.

Frances married widower Fenton Harper in 1860. He died only four years later, taking with him what little wealth Frances had amassed with her writing and speaking thus far. After his death, Frances and her daughter Mary moved back to Philadelphia, where she resumed speaking and teaching.

Later in her life, Frances would say of motherhood,

> Every mother should endeavor to be a true artist. I do not mean by this that every woman should be a painter, sculptor, musician, poet, or writer, but the artist who will write on the tablet of childish innocence thoughts she will not blush to see read in the light of eternity and printed amid the archives of heaven, that the young may learn to wear them as amulets around their hearts and throw them as bulwarks around their lives, and that in the hour of temptation and trial the voices from home may linger around their paths as angels of guidance, around their steps, and be incentives to deeds of high and holy worth.[11]

And despite the fact that her renown as a great writer and orator would far outpace the details that we know of her life as wife and mother, she would say,

> The home may be a humble spot, where there are no velvet carpets to hush your tread, no magnificence to surround your way . . . but what are the costliest gifts of fortune when placed

73

in the balance with the confiding love of dear children or the true devotion of a noble and manly husband whose heart can safely trust in his wife? . . . the crown of her motherhood will be more precious than the diadem of a queen.[12]

She did not despise the work of her home, but neither did she use her home as an excuse not to set her hand to the tasks the Lord had put before her. Though a devoted wife and mother, Frances still managed never to shy away from the hard work of abolition. Her pen was never still.

The Tipping Point

There are many reasons Frances might have gone from humble schoolteacher to renowned lecturer, but the one that tugs at me most has to do with the Fugitive Slave Act of 1850.

The Fugitive Slave Act endangered not only runaway enslaved people seeking sanctuary in northern free states, but also free Black men and women who matched the descriptions of their enslaved counterparts. Maryland furthered this legislation by enacting a law that put any free Black person who entered the state in jeopardy of imprisonment or enslavement.[13] A free man in Frances's own city of Baltimore was kidnapped, sold into slavery, and eventually died before he could regain his freedom.[14]

One theory is that this is the knowledge that galvanized Frances and moved her private support of the Underground Railroad into the public spotlight.

Rather than recoil from the Fugitive Slave Act in fear, Frances spoke all over America—both in the North and the South— offering a rallying cry for change. She did not shrink or shirk but rose to the occasion with everything she could muster. In a letter to William Still, a fellow Black abolitionist, she wrote, "I have a right to do my share of the work. The humblest and feeblest of us can do something; and though I may be deficient in many of the conventionalisms of city life, and be considered as a person of good impulses, but unfinished, yet if there is common rough work to be done, call on me."[15]

Frances's tipping point might have looked a lot like one of mine.

My firstborn son was born the summer of 2016. My husband, Phillip, and I were in the middle of a cross-country move from Minnesota to Mississippi. The lease was up on our cute suburban duplex, and we were staying in a hotel until it was time to set off. Phillip had run out to grab us some food, and I was sitting in bed nursing Wynn and scrolling Facebook.

> Frances's tipping point might have looked a lot like one of mine.

Philando Castile was killed that same day.

I scrolled in horror, processing the details of what had happened. He was shot by a police officer during a traffic stop in the very suburb Phillip and I had been living in for the past year. I immediately called Phillip to check on him, heart hammering in my ears, postpartum hormones rushing through my veins.

Philando Castile's death was not the first such shooting of a Black man that I had ever heard of. It wasn't the first one I had ever mourned. It wasn't even the first one that had happened in a state where I resided.

But it was the first one that felt close. And I remember sitting on that bed, holding my brand-new baby boy, and thinking of how much everything had changed for me. I was now a mother of a little brown-skinned boy. My heart was not only out and about on the streets of Minneapolis in search of takeout, but in my arms.

I do not pretend to know the mind of Frances Harper (would that I did!), but I know what it feels like for something to hit closer to home than ever before. I know what it's like for passion to spark and bleed out onto the page, and for the writing on the page to move one into the lectern. Bronze muse though I may never be, I have mused on so many of the words that Frances shared in myriad speeches, and I have felt the conviction of them deep in my own heart and life.

Frances did not work for fame and renown, but from a deep conviction that the work she was applying herself to was a worthwhile endeavor.

But what I love most about Frances is that her passion for abolition did not just lead her to the speaking circuit—it bubbled over into poetry, and into stirring works of fiction.

If you had asked ten-year-old Jasmine what she wanted to be when she grew up, she would have said, "A teacher and a writer."

At the tender age of thirty, I'm able to apply both of those descriptors to my profession. Except for the fact that, back then, by *teacher* I definitely meant college professor, and by *writer* I most assuredly meant "youngest fiction Pulitzer Prize winner in history."

Since high school seniors make me break out in nervous hives, I doubt that college students are in my future. And I'm already too old to be the youngest Pulitzer Prize winner for fiction. An honest estimation of my fiction-writing skills acknowledges that that prize will forever be out of my reach.

Still, for a Black girl who writes poetry and stories in her spare time, Frances Harper's existence as speaker, mother, poet, and fiction writer is an inspiration and a marvel. It's hard to find a Hallmark Channel Christmas movie about a Black woman, let alone a nineteenth-century novel. And yet, though it is contested that *Iola Leroy* was the first novel published by a Black woman, it was still *one* of the first. Not thirty years after the Civil War, Frances penned a novel about young Iola, a white-passing freedwoman who chose boldly to identify herself as Black rather than to live a life passing for white.

Within the beauty of Frances's storytelling lies the wry cultural commentary that peeks out of her speeches. Before the titular character is even introduced, Frances writes about the religion of the South in tones that echo Frederick Douglass's infamous appendix to his narrative.

> "Oh, I don't take much stock in white folks' religion," said Robert, laughing carelessly.
>
> "The way," said Tom Anderson, "dat some of dese folks cut their cards yere, I think dey'll be as sceece in hebben as hen's teeth. I think wen some of dem preachers brings de Bible 'round an' tells us 'bout mindin our marsters and not stealin' dere tings, dat dey preach to please de white folks, an' dey frows coleness ober de meetin'."[16]

Forty-five years before Zora Neale Hurston famously displayed a penchant for dialect in the 1937 masterpiece, *Their Eyes Were Watching God*, Frances Ellen Watkins Harper's Tom Anderson spoke as Frances herself had heard the formerly enslaved speak during her post-war travels to teach in the South—though his dialect could not disguise his intellect. "*I think*," he said of abusive white masters, "*they'll be as scarce in heaven as hen's teeth*."

For the uninitiated in the ways of southern sayings, that's pretty scarce.

Frances's sentiments echo Douglass's words:

> I love the pure, peaceable, and impartial Christianity of Christ: I therefore hate the corrupt, slaveholding, women-whipping, cradle-plundering, partial and hypocritical Christianity of this land. Indeed, I can see no reason, but the most deceitful one, for calling the religion of this land Christianity. I look upon it as the climax of all misnomers, the boldest of all frauds, and the grossest of all libels.[17]

Throughout *Iola Leroy*, Frances's characters make mention of the difference between true Christianity and the Christianity touted by their enslavers. And Christianity isn't the only hypocrisy *Leroy* dares to address. Says the light-skinned Black soldier Robert, "'Isn't it funny,' said Robert, 'how these white folks look down on colored people, an' then mix up with them?'"[18] and later, "I think that some of these Northern soldiers do two things—hate slavery and hate niggers."[19]

When Iola is introduced, Frances again offers startling cultural commentary. Because Iola is white-passing, it is easy for a white general to be disgusted by the vulnerability of her position as an enslaved woman:

> Could it be possible that this young and beautiful girl had been a chattel, with no power to protect herself from the highest insults that lawless brutality could inflict upon innocent and defenseless womanhood? Could he ever again glory in his American citizenship, when any white man, no matter how coarse, cruel, or brutal, could buy or sell her for the basest purposes? Was it not true that the cause of a hapless people had become entangled with the lightnings of heaven, and dragged down retribution upon the land?[20]

Through her white-passing heroine, Frances forces the reader to acknowledge the value Americans of the period placed on white womanhood over its Black counterpart. Slavery was all fine and good for *Black* women, but the mere thought of a white woman being put in such a vulnerable position was enough to make this white character sick to his stomach.

Frances goes so far as to have Iola reject the marriage proposal of a white doctor who knows her family history—and asks her to hide it in order to live a privileged life as his wife. Iola's own mother had made a similar decision before her, and one could hardly fault the young woman for seeking the protection this white man offered her. But Iola rejects him in favor of maintaining her ties to the Black community and spending the rest of her life working to uplift it.

The magic of *Iola Leroy*, though, isn't in the threads of activism that Frances spins throughout her tale, but in the masterful writing itself. Iola herself is deftly described as "young in years, but old in sorrow; one whom a sad destiny had changed from a light-hearted girl to a heroic woman."[21]

I wonder how much of herself the orphaned, working-class novelist wrote into Iola.

What Frances Teaches Us

Like more than one woman profiled in these pages, Frances Ellen Watkins Harper was raised by a reverend and a teacher. She started working at fourteen and did not stop working until the day she died. She was married only four years before going back to supporting herself and her young daughter. And yet, if single motherhood was a challenge to the calling God placed on her life, Frances kept it to herself. She doggedly pursued her passions—lecturing, writing, and imagining.

I teach at a classical Christian school in Jackson, Mississippi. I'm excited to introduce Frances Ellen Watkins Harper to my students. We are very picky about the classical canon at my school, but we also realize that so many Black voices have been barred from that canon throughout history. Phillis Wheatley is the one Black poet the kids know—maybe Paul Laurence Dunbar, if they're lucky, and later, Langston Hughes. But the canon should be full to bursting with a wide array of Black voices and a huge cross section of the Black experience.

Frances was not just a phenomenal speaker—she was a phenomenal writer. Her poetry and her storytelling abilities have stood the test of time, even when it seemed that time had forgotten them. In fact, just a few years ago, her first published book of poetry, *Forest Leaves*, was rediscovered. For one hundred and fifty years, we assumed that her words were lost forever . . .

and yet they were found by a pesky PhD candidate who knew exactly where to look.

As much as I love playing hide-and-seek with the treasure trove of the influential Black women who have shaped us, it is my earnest hope that fifty years from now, a little Black girl who wants to grow up to be a writer doesn't have to look far to find the work of Frances Ellen Watkins Harper. Perhaps she will have had to memorize *Bible Defense of Slavery* or *The Slave Mother*. Maybe her teacher will have assigned *The Two Offers* in a short story unit. Perhaps in a class that focuses on nineteenth-century literature, *Iola Leroy* will be found in its rightful chronology after Austen and the Brontës.

I do know that my own children and my own students will know her name. And perhaps, now that you've read her words, you can share her brilliance as well.

However, if I have learned anything from Frances, it is that no matter how quiet the record of her brilliance has been kept, it cannot remain silent forever. I did not know about her . . . until I did. And now that I do, I know to be incredibly grateful for her example and influence. And I know that there are myriad women like her, just waiting to be discovered. They are hidden gems and diamonds in the rough now, but they were outspoken dynamos while they lived. And their lives shine as examples to us all.

5

God's Image
Carved in Ebony

Amanda Berry Smith

To say "Thy will be done," from the heart, is more than all burnt offerings and sacrifice; and this prayer prayed from the heart, is what is meant by being entirely and wholly satisfied.

—Amanda Berry Smith

I have often recounted awkward stories of my childhood lot of being the only Black girl in the room. Having grown up in an upper-middle-class evangelical household, I distinctly remember my private-school days. Not only was I always the darkest girl in the room—I was almost always the tallest one, and painfully skinny at that. My mother would often scold me for hunching my shoulders down as far as they could go, trying desperately not to be so noticeable.

Even as an adult, I have to remind myself that it's *okay* to take up space. Though I've been five feet eight inches tall since the age of thirteen or fourteen, my growth stopped there. I am no longer painfully skinny, but sometimes hold pain in the opposite direction as a midsized Black woman in the land of slim-figured Northeast Jackson blondes and brunettes.

During her long and fruitful ministry, Amanda Berry Smith was often the only Black woman in the room. Not only that, but she was also nearly six feet tall. Born into slavery in 1837, she would only receive a combined three months of formal education. She would suffer through two difficult marriages, the deaths of both husbands, and the loss of several children. And yet, in spite of the grief and hardship that colored her life, she would spend her days ministering to others.

Amanda went where God called her to go. A Black American woman in the nineteenth century though she was, she was never dissuaded from God's calling on her life.

Her confidence came not from her status in a world that did not value her womanhood or her ethnicity, but rather, from a deep conviction of God's incredible calling on her life. And ironically, it's *because* of Amanda's singular focus on this calling—the advancement of the Gospel on four continents over a span of fifty years—that history has almost forgotten her.

In the 1998 biography *Amanda Berry Smith: From Washerwoman to Evangelist*, Adrienne M. Israel writes:

> In spite of Smith's contemporary fame, after she died she faded into historical obscurity. No historical biography of her has heretofore been written. Until recently, most scholars excluded her from large biographical collections and church histories. Since African-American history has focused primarily on the political struggle against slavery, segregation, and racial

discrimination, religious figures are rarely discussed unless they founded new denominations or played a major role in political activism. African-American church history is not only a neglected area of study, but what has been written usually emphasizes male leaders, institution building, or the impact of religion on black political and economic history. With the advancing secular age, current scholars rarely write biographies about individuals whose goals and activities have been mainly spiritual rather than political or social. As a result, the important legacy of such figures as Amanda Smith has been overlooked.[1]

More than twenty years after these words were written, they still ring true. While social and political activism offers little assurance that Black women throughout history will be remembered (else Sara G. Stanley and Nannie Helen Burroughs would be names on all of our tongues), a calling that is primarily religious makes that lasting memory even less likely. Picket lines and picket signs are a surer ticket to relevancy than pulpits and a life of service.

Though Amanda's father spent much of her youth aiding runaways on the Underground Railroad, Amanda would grow up to devote herself not to political activism but to the ministry. The strength of her purpose would come from an undivided attention to the calling of Christ.

Humble Beginnings

Amanda was one of Samuel and Mariam Berry's thirteen children and was born in Long Green, Maryland. Her father bought his own freedom when Amanda was a young child, and he worked hard to purchase the freedom of his wife and children. Amanda's freedom was purchased while young; her only memories of her old master's wife were pleasant enough and included frequent visits to the Presbyterian church.

Both of Amanda's parents could read and used the skill to read the Bible to their young family. The first time that a Sunday service made an impact on her, however, was when her wealthy employer, Mrs. Latimer, took her to the Methodist church. Though the teenager was the only Black girl in attendance, a woman took her aside and prayed for her. When she got back home that night, she felt "resolved I would be the Lord's and live for him."[2]

At the age of seventeen, she married Calvin Devine. With Calvin Amanda would have two children and experience the death of her firstborn child. Her second born, Mazie, would be her only child to survive infancy.

Calvin was an unkind husband, often drunk, and he and Amanda endured a rocky marriage until he joined the army during the Civil War. He never returned, freeing Amanda and Mazie to move to Philadelphia and start life again.

In Philadelphia, Amanda met James Smith, with whom she would go on to have three more children, all of whom would die in infancy. Though Amanda and James were married for several years, they lived apart for most of their marriage, since neither of them made enough money to afford accommodations large enough for their small family. James worked as a waiter, sometimes living in the hotels where he worked; Amanda worked as a washerwoman, sometimes lodging near her work sites, and Mazie lived with caretakers. The Smiths lived in squalor, crammed into New York's overcrowded tenements. Two of Amanda's children died of respiratory ailments shortly before their first birthdays.

While James had led Amanda to believe that he wanted to go into the ministry, he spent most of their marriage jockeying for a higher place in the social strata of Black New York. What little money they had was shared with dues for the various social clubs of which he was a member. James's society lifestyle did not mesh with Amanda, who was growing in religious fervor. She would rather host Bible studies in her squalid home, wearing simple Quaker dress, than rub shoulders with Black aristocracy.

During this period, Amanda prayed fervently for sanctification, which she described as "God in you, supplying all your needs according to His riches in glory by Christ Jesus; our need of grace and patience and long suffering and forbearance, for we have to learn how not only to bear, but also to forbear with infirmities of ourselves and others as well."[3]

Amanda was wholly consumed with what it meant to be sanctified, writing, "There is much of human nature for us to battle with, even after we are wholly sanctified, so that we shall ever need the beautiful grace of patience. . . . To say 'Thy will be done,' from the heart, is more than all burnt offerings and sacrifice; and this prayer prayed from the heart, is what is meant by being entirely and wholly satisfied."[4] "Even with my own people, in this country, I have not always met with the pleasantest things. But still I have not backslidden, nor felt led to leave the church. His grace has ever been sufficient. And all we need to-day is to trust Him."[5]

As she wrestled with her desire to grow in the faith, she and James grew further and further apart. In 1869, the year Amanda buried yet another child, James died of stomach cancer.

That same year, Amanda's only living child, Mazie, came to faith, and the two women began traveling to tent meetings across the city, where Amanda began her life's calling as an evangelist.

Sister Preacher

As Amanda's ministry developed, she would find herself in front of mostly white crowds. Their unity in Christ notwithstanding, both Amanda and her daughter often experienced harsh prejudice at these meetings, where confused white crowds wondered what this formerly enslaved woman could have to teach them. Though undaunted in her calling, Amanda was still very much human. She often cried when confronted with outright bigotry.[6] "I do love white folks," Amanda once said, "whether they love me or not, and I want them all saved."[7]

She pressed on, believing she had a message that everyone—Black and white—needed to hear. Providentially, most of her audiences would be white, and later on, when her calling took her to Africa, she would quip, "I find that human nature is the same in Black men, even in Africa, as in white men in America. It is the same old story everywhere: 'None but Jesus can do helpless sinners good.'"[8]

Yet Amanda's ministry in white spaces was headed toward a path that the young washerwoman from Maryland never could have predicted. In July of 1872, she attended a church missions day event at which missionaries from India, China, Japan, and South America shared their experiences overseas. While walking home, Amanda reflected on the fact that she hadn't heard from a single missionary to Africa. She went straight to her room, locked her door, and fell to her knees in prayer: "Lord, Africa's need is great, and I cannot go, though I would like to. But Thou knowest I have no education, and I do not understand geography, so I would not know how to travel."[9]

> "I do love white folks, whether they love me or not, and I want them all saved."

Amanda's prayers would be answered in an unexpected way. Six years later, a woman approached her after a service and told her to pray about going to England. Amanda replied, "Go to England!

Amanda Smith, the colored washerwoman, go to England! No, I am not going to pray a bit; I have to ask the Lord for so many things that I really need, that I am not going to bother Him with what I don't need—to go to England."[10]

The thought lodged in her mind though, and before long, she did go to the Lord in prayer about it:

> "Lord, If Thou dost want me to go to England, make it very clear and help me. I don't know what I would do there, I don't know anybody, but if Thou dost want me, Lord, I leave it all to Thee," and somehow—I can't explain it—but God made it so clear, and put it in my conscience so real and deep, that I could no more doubt that He wanted me to go to England, than I could doubt my own existence.[11]

The Lord opened a door. Amanda set sail for England, planning to stay for three months. She would end up ministering there for twelve years. From England, she would have yet another encounter with a friend who told her to pray about going to a new country: India.

The woman who had lived in squalor in filthy New York tenements—who had lost three children to treatable illnesses and who had been separated from her young daughter in order to work long hours—had been called as a missionary overseas. God opened every door, and Amanda faithfully went through each one. She would arrive in India in 1879 and slowly chart her way to the African mission she had long prayed to visit.

The spiritual landscape of India discouraged the passionate evangelist. "Superstition and idolatry, and infidelity, are so rampant it seems the very air one breathes is impregnated with them."[12] She watched starvation ravage people during a famine, survived a massive landslide, and began to minister to orphan children.

And it is at this juncture—her lifelong mission to orphans—that the symmetry of Amanda Berry Smith's life most inspires me.

Amanda's Love for Sanctification

The retelling of Amanda's life and ministry is far from over, but her dedication to orphan children, first in India, and later in Africa, is one of the most striking aspects of her story.

Amanda was a product of the Holiness movement, a Methodist-led, John Wesley–originated sector of Christianity that was deeply and especially concerned with the theology of *sanctification*. Israel describes it this way:

> [A]fter conversion an earnest Christian would remain "deeply discontent" with "the residues of sin within" and after a time of agonizing soul searching leading to "entire consecration and complete trust," the believer would be purified by God of inward sin and empowered to "live the new life victoriously." Wesley called this experience sanctification, a second crisis when the believer acquired "perfect love." According to Wesley, sanctification could happen as "an instantaneous experience" or could be realized by growth.[13]

Amanda and I differ in church tradition (she a Methodist, and I a Presbyterian), and this difference comes to bear in our view of sanctification. A thorough treatment of those different views is outside of the scope of this text, but Andy Naselli offers a simple primer in his article "Models of Sanctification."[14] However, while Amanda and I disagree on the particulars of sanctification, we definitely agree on its importance.

Sanctification is a thoroughly biblical principle: Romans 15:16, 1 Corinthians 1:2, 6:11, Hebrews 2:11, 10:10, 10:14, and 10:29 all mention a variant of the word itself, but the theme of being molded to the likeness of Christ throughout our Christian walk (Romans 12:1–2) is present throughout the New Testament. And Amanda *yearned* to be molded.

Amanda described sanctification as God's "enduring grace," and prayed that her sufferings would help to sanctify her—to make her more like him.[15]

Her sufferings were so many.

Romans 5:1–5 (ESV, emphasis mine) reads:

> Therefore, since we have been justified by faith, we have peace with God through our Lord Jesus Christ. Through him we have also obtained access by faith into this grace in which we stand, and we rejoice in hope of the glory of God. Not only that, but we **rejoice in our sufferings**, knowing that **suffering produces endurance**, and **endurance produces character**, and **character produces hope**, and hope does not put us to shame, because **God's love has been poured into our hearts through the Holy Spirit** who has been given to us.

Amanda Berry Smith's life is a picture of this passage in action—and evidence of God's answer for her constant prayer of sanctification, of growing more like him.

The woman who was born into slavery, married a cruel husband at seventeen, lost several of her children in their infancy, and lived in poverty and squalor prayed that God would use these things to produce endurance. That endurance produced the character of a woman who prayed fervently to be used by the God that she so desperately wanted to serve. That character produced hope that drove her to the ends of the earth to proclaim the goodness of the God she served. Over one hundred years later, the impact that her life has had on me—can have on you—is proof that this hope did not put her to shame.

I do not pretend to understand the suffering of Amanda Berry Smith. My childhood reads a lot more like Sara G. Stanley's than any other woman's in this book. I was born to privilege, and my life's goal is to use that privilege in a way that glorifies God and upholds the inherent dignity and significance of people who are made in his image.

But I do know what it is like to lose a child. Unlike Amanda, I never held my babies in my arms, but because of the advancement of modern medicine, I knew that I held them in my womb long before she would have known. I got to see their flickering life in pregnancy tests mere days after conception, had access to images of their steady growth in ultrasounds. I watched a heart that was beating furiously one week stare silently back at me from the black-and-white screen the next.

I do not pretend that this is the same grief as losing a ten-month-old son to illness while working my fingers to the bone for eight dollars a week with my husband living elsewhere and my daughter in the care of strangers. I cannot begin to fathom the differences. But I do know how hard it was to be faithful to the Lord with my grief. I do know how hard it was to trust the Lord's purpose to remain sure in spite of my suffering. I do know how hard it is to see God's redemptive blessings in times of grief and loss.

I know the pain of growing up Black in predominately white circles in twenty-first-century America. While I do not downplay that pain, and wrote an entire book about it, I cannot quite compare it to Amanda Berry Smith's role as a nineteenth-century Black woman ministering to white people for a good deal of her life. In *Mother to Son*, I wrote about my hope that my sons would be optimists in spite of a culture that breeds the pain of pessimism. If I had known about Amanda Berry Smith then, I would have held her up as a shining example of exactly the type of optimism I was writing about.

In *Careers Across Color Lines*, Kimberly Hill writes that "Smith argued that God gave her the gift of sanctification at a certain point in her life, and that gift had enabled her to enter ministry despite her gender, limited education, and impoverished background."[16] Amanda also credited that sanctification for her ability to minister in white spaces in spite of the hostility that she often encountered.

While I do not believe that it is possible for a Christian to be perfectly sanctified before they reach heaven's gates, I do see the remarkable pattern of growth that God evidenced in Amanda's life.

The woman who suffered through two hard marriages spent her entire life building up the Bride of Christ.

The woman who lost so many children in infancy spent the second half of her life caring for orphans.

The woman who was born into slavery preached the message of the God who sets the captives free.

The woman who suffered through crippling poverty traveled the world with the Lord supplying every one of her needs.

As God redeemed every area of Amanda's life, she grew more and more like him. The more he strengthened her testimony, the more he strengthened her to his service. There is a beauty there that could so easily be missed by fixating on our theological differences—as there are many. Looking at the life of this sister in Christ, I am humbled by her orthopraxy first, and critical of her orthodoxy second.

> The woman born into slavery preached the message of the God who sets the captives free.

And I will reserve criticism for another space and time, because there is so much to celebrate about God's work in this woman's life.

Amanda and the Motherless

Amanda would finally make it to Africa on January 18, 1882, and would spend the next eight years ministering there. It was in Africa that she would adopt her first orphan, Bob. This adoption and her work with orphans in India would be a catalyst for the ministry she would begin once traveling back to the United States: the Amanda Smith Orphanage and Industrial Home for Abandoned and Destitute Colored Children.

This venture would be funded both by donations and Amanda's own money, which she made through the publishing of her autobiography, *An Autobiography, The Story of the Lord's Dealing with Mrs. Amanda Smith, the Colored Evangelist Containing an Account of Her Life Work of Faith, and Her Travels in America, England, Ireland, Scotland, India, and Africa, as An Independent Missionary.*

If the title seems a mouthful, it is because Amanda led a mouthful of a life. The book is not a short one—it's as thick as any Bible in my house—but it is full of a heart that gave thanks to God for every endeavor she was blessed to encounter.

The orphanage would eventually span an entire city block, and Amanda would write of her goals to "rescue destitute, needy children, especially those of colored parentage," to give them "care, education, and industrial training," and to find them permanent homes.[17]

In 1906, Amanda would undergo deaconess training—the most formal education she had benefited from in her entire life. In 1912, she would leave the care of the orphanage in the hands of others and retire to Florida until her death in 1915.

Amanda's Legacy and Ours

The difficult parts of Amanda's story are not unique to her. The results of the chattel slavery that stain American history, the precarious nature of a woman's place in postindustrial America, the infant mortality rate of impoverished Black children . . . all of these are hardships that many a Black woman in America faced. I would be remiss if I did not point out the fact that so many women have survived and thrived in spite of similar difficulties—difficulties that this twenty-first-century woman can hardly fathom.

I would also be remiss if I did not point out that some of these issues remain rampant in the Black community one hundred years later, and that Black mothers strive to provide stability and hope to their children in spite of these things every single day.

My focus on Amanda isn't meant to paint her struggles as extraordinary, nor even the survival of those struggles. My focus is the same as hers: the God who saw her in the midst of those struggles and used them to move her toward proclaiming his name throughout the world.

Amanda Berry Smith did not claim superpowers. She survived as so many women did—as so many women do—as so many women will. She claimed to serve a powerful God, who helped her not only to survive but to *thrive* in his service against innumerable odds.

Look at the title of her autobiography: *The Lord's Dealing with . . .*

She saw his hand at work in her life in a way that I strive to see his hand at work in mine. She saw his blessing upon her life's work and gave him full glory and honor for everything she was able to accomplish before she died. What a truly beautiful testament to what it means to be a woman of God. We are not called to superhuman strength in any way, shape, form, or fashion. We are merely called to a supernatural faith that he is all too ready to supply us.

When Amanda was a child, she went to the basement of the Quaker home where she worked and begged God for salvation. "If there is such a thing as salvation," she said, "I am determined to have it this afternoon or die."

Israel continues the account:

93

She went to the cellar where she was prepared to stay and die if God did not convert her. On her knees in the basement of this house where she worked as a maid, Smith wrote that she looked up and simply prayed, "O, Lord, if Thou wilt help me, I will believe Thee." At that moment, she said she believed and was converted.[18]

This is not the last time Amanda would beg God to intervene in her life, nor the last time she would see his answer so clearly. If Elizabeth Freeman teaches us to listen and stand up for ourselves—if Sara G. Stanley teaches us to advocate fiercely for others—if Nannie Helen Burroughs teaches us to be radically consistent—if Frances Ellen Watkins Harper teaches us to use our creativity in powerful ways—then Amanda Berry Smith teaches us, simply, to pray. To trust. To obey.

Of all the lessons we have learned so far, it seems the simplest. And yet we see the results in such a mighty way in Amanda's life, and struggle to trust those results so much in our own, that I think we know better. This washerwoman turned evangelist is the least educated woman we have learned about so far—and yet the most well-traveled of the bunch. The Lord took her to the ends of the earth to share his Gospel and gave her a testimony that resonates through the annals of history to this day.

Let it resonate with you. And pray to be used mightily by him.

6

Mother from Far Away

Maria Fearing

What could this woman of fifty-six years, and with less than a high school education, do in that darkest of all the continents, where she would be compelled to learn the unwritten language of the native people?

—said of Maria Fearing

I will never forget my first trip to Zambia.

My parents and most of my siblings had been living in the country for over a year by the time my husband and I packed up our young son and made the trek across the ocean. Phillip had been to Zambia and other African countries before, but this was my very first trip to the motherland. I am a nervous flyer, and the twenty-four-hour-plus journey had my stomach in knots. Yet I was excited to see my family after so much time apart and thrilled to step onto the continent my ancestors unwillingly sailed from so many generations ago.

Africa is vast. Our modern-day maps hardly do it justice. It is a continent *three times* the size of the United States, filled with a diverse array of countries, languages, and customs. Countries we think of as being neighbors are hundreds of miles apart. People we think of as a monolith exist in myriad people groups.

When I visited Zambia, I knew I was close to Victoria Falls and the lifelong ministry of David Livingstone, the famous British missionary. But I had no idea that I was just a stone's throw away from the Democratic Republic of the Congo, where Maria Fearing spent much of her life ministering to Congolese orphans.

The names of Black female missionaries have become a well-trodden pathway in my mind lately. Betsey Stockton, a formerly enslaved Presbyterian woman, was the first single American woman (Black or white) to become a missionary, and many Black women would follow in her footsteps. Amanda Berry Smith's is a story that we've already told, but Fanny Jackson Coppin, Althea Brown Edmiston, Lulu Fleming, Nora A. Gordon, and others would follow in Betsey's footsteps.

Maria Fearing was born into slavery in Alabama. In 1838, the year she was born, it was illegal to teach either enslaved or free people of color how to read. By the time of her death in 1937, she would have a hand in helping to bring the Gospel— including a Bible in the Baluba-Lulua language—to the Congo. Born into the unjust institution of American chattel slavery, she would spend half of her adult life championing the cause of the orphans who would call her "Mamu Fearing" or "Mama wa Mputu" (Mother from Far Away).

David Livingstone was a giant among missionaries—a man worthy of remembrance. Gladys Aylward, Amy Carmichael, and Mary Slessor are all women whose names should inspire us to praise the Lord for the work he accomplished through them.

Maria Fearing belongs on that illustrious list.

Daughter of the South

We have spoken of Elizabeth Freeman's quest for freedom—of Frances Ellen Watkins Harper's fear of the Fugitive Slave Law—of the slavery that was part of Amanda Berry Smith's childhood. But in Maria, we have a unique picture of slavery as it was about to let out its dying breath in America. This breath would not come peacefully, but rather as the result of the bloodiest war in U.S. history.

Elizabeth Freeman represents a time in America when the North was still grappling with how to relate to its enslaved population. Hers and similar suits for freedom would begin to shape northern slave laws, leading to the abolition of the institution in many states. Yet with the expansion of the United States into new territories and the economic boom that was the cotton industry, the eradication of slavery in the South became a more and more distant possibility. By the time Dred Scott sued for his freedom in the mid 1800s, the issue of slavery had become so tense that a case he might have won fifty years before was an impossible victory.

A full treatment of the ills of American chattel slavery is outside of the scope of this chapter. I do not want to spend the precious time I have talking about Maria Fearing lambasting the so-called "peculiar institution" that enslaved her. However, Maria's story is even more astonishing set against the backdrop of the culture into which she was born.

Christianity was often used as an excuse to keep people like Maria Fearing in chains. Bible verses taken out of context were applied to her predicament as "proof" that the God of the once-enslaved Israelites was not offended by the institution. It is important to note that while the word *slavery* is mentioned in the Bible, the chattel slavery practiced in America was an entirely different beast.

First, chattel slavery started—always—with manstealing. That is, taking a person from their home and importing them to a new country with the express purpose of using them for hard labor.

Scripture clearly states, "Whoever steals a man and sells him, and anyone found in possession of him, shall be put to death" (Exodus 21:16 ESV).

Second, chattel slavery was both race-based and hereditary. There is no precedent, either in Old Testament law or in Roman law, for a slavery that is race-based *and* hereditary. In fact, the Old Testament makes a way for the enslaved to be freed in sabbath and Jubilee years (see Exodus 21, Leviticus 25, and Deuteronomy 15).[1]

Third, chattel slavery not only denied the brotherhood of all of mankind, but specifically barred the enslaved from participating in full Christian brotherhood with their masters. Prior to the eighteenth century, it was encouraged *not* to teach enslaved people about Christianity because it was widely believed that an enslaved person who had become a believer—and therefore a sibling in Christ—could no longer be kept in slavery (see Katharine Gerbner's *Christian Slavery*). This is similar to God's law of Leviticus 25:39, which bars the Israelites from making their kinsmen slaves (eighteenth-century Americans largely viewed themselves as a new Israel, bound by the blood of Christ).[2]

It is tempting to some to try to downplay the cruelty of American slavery, to think that *some* masters were cruel to their slaves, certainly, but *lots* of slaves were very happy and well cared for. The cruelty of American chattel slavery is well documented. The separation of families, the rape of women, the dismemberment of men, and the complete stripping of legal recourse against these actions is well documented both socially and legislatively. This is not to mention the cruelty of the Middle Passage. The fact that some masters were kind to those they enslaved is of no consequence, because *legislatively*, they had little inducement to be kind, and therefore, legislatively, there were people of the United States who were both (1) barred from citizenship and (2) barred from the protection of citizenship enjoyed by others.

The citizenship piece is an important one. Because Black Americans were considered by many not to be citizens of the United States (nor, if we remember Supreme Court Chief Justice Roger B. Taney's argument, even *eligible* for future citizenship regardless of their freedom status), they existed in a bit of a legislative purgatory. They had to rely on the kindness of actual (white) American citizens to advocate for their rights.

And there were, indeed, citizens who advocated on behalf of the enslaved. It's important to note that the distaste of slavery is not a modern phenomenon. *While* Black image-bearers were living their lives in chains, so many voices cried out on their behalf. James Otis Jr., Anthony Benezet, Granville Sharp, John Wesley, James Ramsay, Josiah Wedgwood, and so many others used their voices to advocate for the enslaved.

Quakers, especially, were well documented in their disapproval of slavery, and the religious movement was far from silent during the founding of the United States. American slaveowners also had access to the personal accounts of the formerly enslaved—like Phillis Wheatley and Olaudah Equiano, the latter of whom detailed extensively the cruelty of slavery that he witnessed with his own eyes—as well as those who had escaped, like Frederick Douglass.

Again, I do not want to use this space to belabor the ills of chattel slavery—not because I do not think those evils should be consistently exposed, but because I do not want to distract from Maria Fearing's tale. However, it is important to understand that this woman was born into a cruel institution that denied her even the right to read.[3] I do not write these truths to make much of American chattel slavery but to make much of the God who intervened.

Humble Beginnings to a Brave End

Maria Fearing was born into chattel slavery in Alabama in 1838. Raised on the Oak Hill Plantation, she was trained as a house girl. Maria spent her early years taking care of children, learning to cook, clean, and mend, and excelling at all things domestic under the care of her Presbyterian master's wife, Mrs. Winston. Because of Mrs. Winston, Maria was raised in the faith and was taught Bible verses, catechism, and stories of missionary adventures in Africa.

> Maria was born into a cruel institution that denied her even the right to read.

Althea Edmiston, a Black missionary in the Congo who was well acquainted with Maria Fearing and her influence there (and could have easily commanded an entire chapter in this text) wrote a biography of Maria that I will reference most often throughout this chapter.

"The stories of Africa especially touched the heart of little Maria, and she said, 'I will go to Africa some day if I can.' Thus, without the slightest realization of it, this lowly little girl was being wonderfully and beautifully trained for a work for which God had, no doubt, chosen her even before her birth."[4]

At the age of twenty-seven, shortly after the end of the Civil War, Maria Fearing was set free. She used the domestic skills she had learned while enslaved to earn a living. Maria set her sights on two ambitions that would have seemed impossible for a young girl growing up in slavery in Alabama: to learn to read and to own her own home.

She accomplished both feats, first buying her home (notable for any woman of her time, let alone a Black one), and then, at the age of thirty-three, entering school. She was the only adult pupil in her class but humbled herself and learned alongside the children. Within a few years, she would become a teacher at the same school where she had learned.

It was at this school that Maria first met William Henry Sheppard, a Black missionary who came to give an address about his harrowing adventures overseas.

Edmiston writes,

> Maria was one of his most attentive listeners. The little spark that had been kindled in her heart years and years before, through the hearing of the story of the "little naked, bare-footed heathen children in Africa," told by Mrs. Winston, burst into an uncontrollable flame, and she at once offered her service.[5]

Maria was already fifty-six years old at this point in her life and was rejected by the mission board because of her advanced age. However, with the same determination that had led her to purchase her own home and learn to read after the age of thirty, Maria decided to finance her own journey.

She sold her home and moved away from everything she knew, and on May 26, 1894, she arrived in New York to set sail for Africa.

Once she arrived on the continent, she would follow a guide twelve hundred miles on foot to Sheppard's mission in the Congo. She went from her humble home in Alabama to an even humbler home there, with dirt floors and thatched roofs. Undeterred by her new surroundings, Maria would begin to learn the new language and make a home in this new environment, eventually founding the Pantops Home for Girls.

At first, this home was financed completely by Maria herself. The country was in the midst of political upheaval as King Leopold II of Belgium fought for control.

There were many uprisings and attacks against the government officials, who were trying to police the country. In all these disturbances the missionaries, too, stood in danger of losing their lives. One day news reached the Mission station that the native soldiers, armed with modern rifles, had mutinied; that they had killed the trader just across the river, and were coming to attack the missionaries. There was much excitement. The girls, weeping, gathered around Miss Fearing. She read to them part of the ninety-first Psalm, and told them to pray, and that she also would pray. . . . God heard and answered, and the soldiers did not come.[6]

Maria Fearing was no stranger to slavery. She herself had been born into chains. Yet the slavery that the Belgians exacted upon their Congolese captives was of a different breed than American chattel slavery. In America, enslaved people were seen as a commodity to be maintained and protected;[7] in Belgian-controlled Congo, they were seen as expendable.

The Belgians exploited the Congolese laborers in an effort to mine as much rubber as possible. When the enslaved did not meet the exacting quotas, they were punished with the removal of limbs or the death of their children. The removal of hands became so synonymous with Belgian rule that there are countless pictures of missionaries posing with handless children (including one such image of William Sheppard). Sheppard was one of many missionaries who wrote home to report the cruelty to which the Congolese were subjected.

The most defenseless victims of this conflict were the children Maria sought to minister to. Seen as not only a valuable source of labor but also as a source of manpower for King Leopold's army, these children were preyed upon by Leopold's regime. On April 27, 1890, the king wrote,

We must set up three children's colonies. One in the Upper Congo near the equator, specifically military, with clergy for

religious instruction and for vocational education. One at Leo-
poldville under clergy with a soldier for military training. One
at Boma like that at Leo. . . . The aim of these colonies is above
all to furnish us with soldiers. We thus have to build three big
barracks at Boma, Leo, and near the equator . . . each capable
of housing 1500 children and administrative personnel.[8]

These children's colonies grew numerous. Some of them
were even manned by Catholic missionaries who, unlike their
Protestant counterparts, were loyal to King Leopold. The con-
ditions in the colonies were so abysmal that the children living
there had only a 50 percent survival rate.[9]

Contrasting the terror of an orphan's life under the rule of
King Leopold to the safety that Maria and others at her mission provided offers an even deeper glimpse into the bravery of
those called to service in the Congo.

Maria worked tirelessly on behalf of these young girls, teaching them the same domestic skills she was taught in her youth,
and discipling them in much the same way Mrs. Winston had
discipled her. Pantops became a home for more than forty children, as well as a respite for young girls whose parents allowed
them to go and learn from Maria.

Twelve years into doing this work, Maria would have to return home on furlough because of her health. However, when
she returned to the mission the next time, she was funded by
the Presbyterian church, which saw all of the good that Miss
Fearing was accomplishing.

And Miss Fearing she was called. The woman who had been
born into slavery in Alabama was part of the very first integrated Presbyterian mission in the Congo, and she was afforded
a respect by her missionary peers that she never could have
imagined back home.

Again Maria's health began to wane, and she went back
to the United States. She wrote to the committee after she

recovered, asking once again to be sent to the Congo, to her girls:

> As the good Committee knows that my heart is bound up in the work of Congoland, especially at Luebo, I must say it is very hard on me, though it is meant in all love and kindness to me. My hopes are all blasted for the future. Please my dear Committee, take me in your prayers before the Throne of Grace, that I may not be rebellious against the thing that is best for me, your humble servant. I was, and still am hoping to be allowed to unburden the Committee with the expense of taking me to Africa again. I have given much prayer to this subject. I ask the Committee to do what they think is best for me. I am much grieved over the matter.[10]

Maria was not to return to the Congo, however, as a woman nearing ninety; her body was too fragile to make the trip. Yet, even as her petition was denied, the committee said of her,

> She has been modest, faithful, conscientious, and devoted. She has been universally kind and loving in times of need, and all of us will miss her gentle ministrations of love and thoughtfulness. But above all we believe that her work will not only live in the lives of the girls she has trained in the Pantops Home, but it will endure through many generations in their descendants.[11]

Maria died in 1937 at the age of ninety-nine. She never married and never bore children, but she was Mother from Far Away to scores of Congolese children, and devoted her life to the service of others.

Meeting Women Like Maria

While I was learning about Maria Fearing, I took a deep dive into the Black women who had served as missionaries throughout the late nineteenth and early twentieth centuries. I had no idea how many names I would find. Would there be ten names I had never heard of? Twenty? Fifty?

On one list alone, I found more than *eighty*.[12]

More than eighty Black women who—from the height of chattel slavery to the birth of the Jim Crow south—undertook the incredible journey and responsibility of bringing the Gospel to foreign lands. While their own homeland saw them as less than human—less worthy of protection, less worthy of citizenship, less worthy of rights—they used what resources they had to bring the message of their citizenship in heaven.

The list of Presbyterian missionaries alone is full of precious names: Mrs. James Priest, Mary Lepien, Mrs. Harrison Ellis, Louise Coke, Mrs. Edward Wilmot Blyden, Lucy Gantt Sheppard (William's wife), Lillian Thomas DeYampert, Althea Brown Edmiston (author of the oft-referenced biography of Maria Fearing), Annie Katherine Taylor Rochester, Hulda Claudine Blamoville, and Mrs. Susan Underhill.[13]

Here is a list of Black Baptist women who served in the Congo: Dr. Louise (Lulu) Fleming, Nora A. Gordon, Clara Howard, Mrs. John Ricketts, and Mrs. Eva Boone.[14]

There were also Methodist, Brethren, Seventh Day Adventist, African Methodist Episcopal, Episcopal, and others represented. They ministered in Liberia, South Africa, Angola, Sierra Leone, Malawi, Nigeria, Cameroon, and Ghana. They ministered from the early 1800s into the twentieth century.

And then the names begin to peter out. As segregation's stranglehold in America tightened, Black missionary advancement lessened. And now, in 2020, I have had more than one person ask me why we "have never had Black missionaries."

Oh, but we have. We have had so very many. Though their names are not usually on the top of easily accessible lists, the lists exist. Like Maria's, their legacies exist, even when we don't have the means to find them.

When I first set out to learn about Maria, I found myself at a loss. I started my research the way I normally do: Googling for dissertations. As I read about the influence of Maria and other missionaries, I mined the footnotes for as much information as I could find about her. Every source had one book in common: *Maria Fearing: A Mother to African Girls*, by Althea Brown Edmiston.

I searched high and low for a copy of this book—a pamphlet that now exists as a single chapter in a broader volume about Presbyterian missionaries in the Congo. Every copy I found cost upward of two hundred dollars, and I wasn't at a point in my research where I could spend that amount of money. I reached out to several colleges that had the book in their libraries, trying to see if I could get photocopied pages from the source, but COVID-19 made a difficult task even more difficult, and I kept hitting a wall.

In the foreword of *Mother to Son*, I write about Karen Ellis and the fact that she was instrumental in the topic of my last book. I reached out to her in frustration over my dilemma and quipped, "It's funny—Althea Brown Edmiston wrote the book."

Karen happens to be the director of the Edmiston Center for the Study of the Bible and Ethnicity—named for Althea and her husband, Alonzo, themselves missionaries to the Congo. The center resides on the Atlanta campus of Reformed Theological Seminary, where my husband, Phillip, is an institutional vice president. I had actually met Althea's descendants at the opening of the center earlier in the year, before the idea for this book even fully materialized.

Karen arranged for the center to purchase the book, and I stopped by RTS Atlanta during an unrelated business trip to read it. I opened the volume and learned from Althea about Maria. And, as I did every time my hard work ended in a source that told me everything I could ever dream of knowing about one of these women, I cried.

The Lord's hand was on my meeting with Maria from the beginning.

The Lord's Hand

Maria's story was my gateway into countless other stories of Black female missionaries who spent their lives sharing the Gospel of Christ in distant lands. The Lord's hand was on her story—on so many other stories.

And his hand was on *my* story, in all of the ways it intersected with Maria's. He is not limited by America's painful legacy of chattel slavery. He was not limited by Maria Fearing's illiteracy. He was not limited by her age. He was not limited by her infirmity. His power shone all the more because of the limits mankind's cruelty placed on her, his grace in her salvation shone all the more in her dogged pursuit of ministry in spite of her origins.

> God is not limited by America's painful legacy of chattel slavery—and was not limited by Maria's illiteracy.

Maria could have grown up hating the Christianity that was often used as an excuse to enslave her. Instead, she thanked the Lord for the ability to walk in freedom and used her entire life to offer eternal freedom to others.

God is not silent. Even when it seems as though an entire country is blind to his commands, he still preserves a remnant for his glory. Even when an institution is as anti-Gospel as American chattel slavery, the Lord can preserve a heart and focus it on Gospel service.

Maria Fearing wanted such simple things in life: a home, an education, a ministry to others. The fact that chattel slavery threatened to make those impossible should wound and humble us.

At this writing, I have spent almost two years owning my first home. I am the same age Maria was when she first learned how to read, and I have been afforded all of the education that I could desire. The ministry God has called me to is constantly at my fingertips in the lives of my own children and others.

I am humbled by God's grace in the life of Maria Fearing, and the way that grace has trickled down into my own life by beholding her legacy.

Around the same time that I was writing Maria's story, I was reading 1 Chronicles. In the midst of myriad male-dominated genealogies, a woman's name stood out to me: Sheerah. Sitting quietly in 1 Chronicles 7:24 are the seemingly innocuous words "His daughter was Sheerah, who built Lower and Upper Beth-horon and Uzzen-sheerah."

That's it. That's all we get. In the midst of sons after sons after sons, we hear about one daughter, and all we get to learn about her is that she built two cities. She is not listed in the genealogy because of who she bore or who she married—but because of what she *built*.

There are innumerable purposes for biblical genealogies, but honing in on the historical purpose, I am struck by the similarity of seeing Sheerah's name in the midst of that list and seeing Maria's or Lucy's or Hulda's or Louise's name in a long list of missionaries. All that I will ever know about most of these women is that they built. They built Gospel legacies that remain largely unsung, that might be lost in a long list of names we gloss over every day to get to the juicier stories in the narrative.

But God is at work even in the names we pass over. And I am so grateful that he didn't allow me to pass over Maria Fearing's.

7

Where Are Our Illustrious Ones?

Maria Stewart

What if I am a woman; is not the God of ancient times the God of these modern days?

—Maria Stewart

I was raised to be very defensive of America's legacy.

There were an ungrateful people, I was taught, who stood poised to defame the name of the nation that had birthed me. In their quest to right the wrongs of my ancestral home, they were going a step *too far*, sullying the legacy of this great nation by questioning her morality—her worthiness as the crown jewel that deserved the title of world superpower.

My parents meant well. They were, after all, raising me in a nation where I am free to praise the name of Christ—a luxury that Christians throughout history haven't had the privilege of claiming. America is a rich nation. America is a promising nation. America is a young and inventive nation.

And America, I was taught, for all of her flaws, is at her heart, a *Christian* nation.

It wasn't until adulthood, armed, ironically, with the tools that these same parents gave me to dive deep into primary sources and read them for exactly what they are, that I began to question these mantras. *Was* America a Christian nation? Had it always been understood as such by all of its residents? And as a descendant of the enslaved, was I the inheritor of a legacy that saw America in this shining light?

I must answer *no*. And I do not answer that standing in the ranks of the critical race theorists the Church so intensely opposes (and often fears) at this moment in history—or the secular humanists, Marxists, or other "ists" that I personally was taught to fear in times past. I stand in the line of a very well-documented prophetic legacy, peppered not only with men like Frederick Douglass but women like Maria Stewart.

And men like the one who inspired her: David Walker.

In 1829, David Walker wrote *David Walker's Appeal to the Colored Citizens of the World*. In this stirring appeal, Walker—himself a Christian—lambasted his own Christian nation for participating in the barbarous trade of chattel slavery and called an entire nation to repentance. Wasting no time, he launches into his preamble:

> Having travelled over a considerable portion of these United States, and having, in the course of my travels, taken the most accurate observations of things as they exist—the result of my observations has warranted the full and unshaken conviction, that we, (coloured people of these United States,) are the most

degraded, wretched, and abject set of beings that ever lived since the world began; and I pray God that none like us ever may live again until time shall be no more. They tell us of the Israelites in Egypt, the Helots in Sparta, and of the Roman Slaves, which last were made up from almost every nation under heaven, whose sufferings under those ancient and heathen nations, were, in comparison with ours, under this enlightened and Christian nation, no more than a cypher—or, in other words, those heathen nations of antiquity, had but little more among them than the name and form of slavery; while wretchedness and endless miseries were reserved, apparently in a phial, to be poured out upon our fathers, ourselves and our children, by *Christian Americans!*[1]

Walker continues to call for judgment against the United States for her participation in this enterprise, as other nations—both past and present—have been judged:

All persons who are acquainted with history, and particularly the Bible, who are not blinded by the God of this world, and are not actuated solely by avarice—who are able to lay aside prejudice long enough to view candidly and impartially, things as they were, are, and probably will be—who are willing to admit that God made man to serve Him *alone,* and that man should have no other Lord or Lords but Himself—that God Almighty is the *sole proprietor* or *master* of the WHOLE human family, and will not on any consideration admit of a colleague, being unwilling to divide his glory with another—and who can dispense with prejudice long enough to admit that we are *men,* notwithstanding our *improminent noses* and *woolly heads,* and believe that we feel for our fathers, mothers, wives and children, as well as the whites do for theirs.[2]

If Walker's words sound familiarly prophetic, it is because he speaks in the style of the American jeremiad—so named for the prophet Jeremiah, who wept as he prophesied judgment on the nation of Israel for her idolatry and injustice against the vulnerable. Walker was part of a movement that applied this jeremiad style to distinctly Black American woes and issues, and through his work and others', the African American jeremiad was born.

If Walker's eventual calls for the enslaved to free themselves from the bonds that restrained them by any means necessary sound radical to you, consider that Walker resided in a nation where the Declaration of Independence claimed that mankind has a *right* and a *duty* to do just that.

If Walker's speech against "the whites" makes you uncomfortable, I ask that you take into account the well-documented speech against Walker's ethnicity that he is responding to:

Have they not, after having reduced us to the deplorable condition of slaves under their feet, held us up as descending originally from the tribes of *Monkeys* or *Orang- Outangs?* O! my God! I appeal to every man of feeling—is not this insupportable? Is it not heaping the most gross insult upon our miseries, because they have got us under their feet and we cannot help ourselves? Oh! pity us we pray thee, Lord Jesus, Master.[3]

Walker's language is forceful. To any white contemporary guilty of the sins that he outlines it would be frightful. But it is no more forceful than the language of the prophets of old. And if we truly believe that American chattel slavery was an evil institution—and the eyewitness accounts of so many enslaved Americans tell us that we *must* believe that, no matter what our modern historical gymnastics demand of us—then what other language could possibly be *more* appropriate than the language of judgment and repentance?

Before Black liberation theology was codified—while Karl Marx was still a young man, before critical race theory was a twinkle in Gramscian Marxism's eye—David Walker lambasted the so-called Christian nation of America based sheerly on his understanding of God's Word. I will leave the critique of his work for another text—as there are, indeed, things to criticize— but the point I'm making is this: "I call God, I call Angels, I call men to witness, that the destruction of the Americans is at hand, and will be speedily consummated unless they repent," Walker urges, and, "But Oh Americans! Americans!! I warn you in the name of the Lord, (whether you will hear, or forbear,) to repent and reform, or you are ruined!!!"[4]

With these words, Walker galvanized an entire generation of activists. And one of those activists is the subject of this chapter—credited with being the first American woman of any ethnicity to give public speeches to crowds of men and women, both Black and white: Maria W. Stewart.

Birth of a Speechmaker

Maria Stewart was born in Connecticut in 1803. By the time she was five years old, both of her parents had died, leaving Maria to fend for herself as the indentured servant of a clergyman for the next decade. Before Maria left, she would begin the slow work of teaching herself how to read in the clergyman's extensive library.

At fifteen, Maria left to become a maid. It was during this period that she took advantage of the local Sabbath schools and started to piece together more of an education for herself. It was also through Sabbath school that Maria continued her religious education, although her dramatic conversion was a few years off yet.

In 1826, Maria married James Stewart, a comfortably wealthy veteran of the War of 1812. It was by James's side that she joined the Black middle class of Boston, Massachusetts. Just three years after their marriage, however, James died, and white executors cheated Maria out of the money from his will. Once again, the young woman found herself destitute.

At this point, she began writing for William Lloyd Garrison's famous abolitionist magazine, *The Liberator*. In 1831, she began giving her first public addresses.

Maria's public addresses are notable for several reasons. First, she spoke in the rhetorical style of the African American jeremiad, which she had been inspired to perfect from her reading of David Walker, whom she called a "most noble, fearless, and undaunted" man.[5]

David Walker's speech can be understood as an outworking of the tradition of the African American jeremiad, particularly in his calls for the repentance of white America. While many historians focus on the more radical aspects of Walker's speech—that is, his call for Black Americans to take their freedom by any means necessary—they sometimes neglect to hold space for his clarion call to white America, beseeching white Americans to atonement. "O Americans! Americans!! I call God—I call angels—I call men, to witness, that your DESTRUCTION *is at hand*, and will be speedily consummated unless you REPENT."[6]

And it is in the spirit of David Walker that Maria felt herself moved to speak, not just because of care for her countrymen, but in response to the call of the Gospel on her life.

> And truly, I can say with St. Paul, that at my conversion, I came to the people in the fulness of the gospel of grace. Having spent a few months in the city of _____, previous, I saw the flourishing condition of their churches and the progress they were making in their Sabbath Schools. I visited their Bible Classes and heard of the union that existed in their Female Associations. On my arrival here, not finding scarce an individual who felt interested in these subjects, and but few of the whites, except Mr. Garrison, and his friend Mr. Knapp; and hearing that those gentlemen had observed female influence was powerful, my soul became fired with a holy zeal for your cause; every nerve

and muscle in me was engaged in your behalf. I felt that I had a great work to perform; and was in haste to make a profession of my faith in Christ, that I might be about my Father's business.[7]

Maria's call to speak on behalf of her Black brethren, then, flowed out of her calling as a woman of God. We cannot understand Maria's zeal for equality without understanding her zeal for the Gospel. Her understanding that she was created in God's image bolstered her bold calls for white America to make space for its Black brethren:

Many thinks, because your skins are tinged with a sable hue, that you are an inferior race of beings; but God does not consider you as such. He hath formed and fashioned you in his own glorious image, and hath bestowed upon you reason and strong powers of intellect. He hath made you to have dominion over the beasts of the field, the fowls of the air, and the fish of the sea. He has crowned you with glory and honor; hath made you but a little lower than the angels; and, according to the Constitution of these United States, he hath made all men free and equal.[8]

It is important to note that for those prone to religious fervor over American exceptionalism, the Constitution and the Declaration of Independence are sacred texts. Elizabeth Freeman has already exhibited the importance of the wording of the Declaration in her freedom suit, and many Black Americans would follow suit.

However, by Maria's first speech in 1831, a new movement was taking shape in America. Not only were enslaved Black people systemically subjugated—their free counterparts were seen as a problem that no white American wanted to deal with. Various movements to send free Black Americans to colonies in Africa—a continent most had never set foot on in their entire lives—were cropping up all over the country. Several states had laws barring free Black men and women from entering their borders. Notably, as the country expanded westward, the question of slavery wasn't the only one politicians grappled with; northerners who did not want enslaved Black people on the western front often didn't want *free* Black people there either.

Maria, David, and, as we have already mentioned, Frances, found themselves in a nebulous no-man's-land. Not enslaved, but not quite free—not citizens, but not bondsmen—they were left to forge an unlikely path to make space for themselves in the American dream.

And make space they did. Though Walker died not long after his famous (and infamous) pamphlet was circulated, Maria took up the mantle for three years, speaking far and wide on behalf of not only enslaved Black people but free Black men and women as well.

Maria was one of the foremothers of Black female use of the jeremiad, predating Frances Harper by several years. In *Origins of the African American Jeremiad*, Willie J. Harrell Jr. writes, "In the discourse of Black women Jeremiahs, a number of universal themes materialized: the sexual mistreatment of slave women by white men and the effect slavery had on slave mothers; the optimism for constructing a coalition between Black and white women; and the call for Black community uplift (Yee, Black Women Abolitionists 122)."[9]

On these points, Maria never faltered. In her speech "Religion and the Pure Principles of Morality," she hit on three of them: the sexual mistreatment of slave women, motherhood, and the call for Black community uplift.

"Dark and dismal is the cloud that hangs over thee," she cried out to white American listeners, "for thy cruel wrongs and injuries to the fallen sons of Africa. The blood of her murdered ones cries to heaven for vengeance against thee. Thou art almost become drunken with the blood of her slain; thou hast enriched thyself through her toils and labors; and now thou refuseth to make even a small return. And thou hast caused the daughters of Africa to commit whoredoms and fornications; but upon thee be their curse."[10]

And, "O, ye mothers, what a responsibility rests on you! You have souls committed to your charge, and God will require a strict account of you. It is you that must create in the minds of your little girls and boys a thirst for knowledge, the love of virtue, the abhorrence of vice, and the cultivation of a pure heart."[11]

And, finally, "O, ye daughters of Africa, awake! awake! arise! no longer sleep nor slumber, but distinguish yourselves. Show forth to the world that ye are endowed with noble and exalted faculties. O ye daughters of Africa!"[12]

Maria was unflinching in her resolve to speak as much truth as she possibly could. Her rhetorical skill paved the way for other Black women to follow along in her footsteps, adding their voices to the movement. Though Maria would only speak for three years, she packed a lifetime of passionate exhortation into that short window.

The Illustrious Ones

Maria once asked of her audience, "Where are the names of *our* illustrious ones?"[13] speaking of the lack of renowned Black voices. Little did Mrs. Stewart realize that her voice would be one of the most illustrious in the history of the oratory tradition in which she participated.

After three years of devoting herself to the cause of racial uplift, Maria retired and became a public school teacher for many years. In 1878, just a year before her death, she would finally receive a widow's pension for her husband's service in the War of 1812, and she used her earnings to publish her speeches and writings. Maria died in 1879, after making her writings available to the world.

Sometimes, it is easier for us to look in wonder at the life of women like the other Maria—Maria Fearing. We understand the limitations of being born into slavery. We can see the impressive ascent from enslaved woman to homeowner to self-financed missionary quite clearly. It is more difficult for us to understand the fact that enslaved Black people were not the only oppressed Black people in America.

For instance, in Alabama, the fine for teaching an enslaved woman like Maria Fearing to read was *exactly the same* as the fine for teaching a free woman like Maria Stewart to read. In some states, enslaved people could not testify against their masters; during David Walker's free upbringing, free Black people were not allowed to testify against white people. There were entire states that would bar Maria Stewart entry because she was not an enslaved woman, and free Black Americans were not welcome within their borders. Not to mention the fact that Maria was cheated out of her husband's money and forced back into destitution by white swindlers.

The blocking of Black citizenship in America was not limited to enslaved Black people. While I intend to make no comparison between being owned as human chattel and being born in freedom, I do want the reader to understand that both statuses were at the bottom of the totem pole of the American caste system. Women like Sara G. Stanley and Charlotte Forten Grimké (the Daughter of a Legacy in chapter 9) are remarkable in part because their privileged upbringings were a rarity, not a norm. Maria Stewart, Nannie Helen Burroughs, and Amanda Berry Smith had the childhoods that more closely resembled the experience of the majority of free Black youth.

Imagine the desperation of being free . . . and yet having no legal recourse to protect one from being kidnapped and taken into slavery because the Fugitive Slave Law demanded a warm body to take the place of a runaway. Imagine the desperation of being free . . . and yet having limited prospects for advancement because there were certain states where Black people simply were not allowed to live. Imagine the desperation of being free . . . and yet living in a nation where Supreme Court Justice Roger B. Taney argued that *no* Black person—be he an enslaved Black person or the descendant of enslaved Black people—was afforded protection under the Constitution.

It is against this desperation that Maria leveled her jeremiads, calling for the nation that claimed to be a city on a hill to *act like it*, or to face the wrath of the God it claimed to serve.

God Don't Like Ugly

Here's my problem: I am too nice.

I don't think I could ever stand up and rail against the wicked establishment the way Maria Stewart did. The voice of my southern upbringing would haunt me in my dreams, telling me to be respectful, to be docile, to know my place. "You catch more flies with honey than with vinegar," after all.

But in the spirit of the prophets of old, Maria was not worried about her words being palatable to her listeners. She was bound by her understanding of the implications of the Gospel to advocate for the most vulnerable members of the society she inhabited. She was convinced—and rightfully so—that God was not pleased with the injustice rampant in America, and she aimed to use her voice to call out that injustice for the ugliness that it was.

> Maria called for the nation that claimed to be a city on a hill to **act like it**.

I want to learn to do the same. I know it will be an uphill battle for a young woman who is given to timidity, but I want to try. If Maria Stewart could go from illiterate adult stumbling along in Sabbath school to being credited as the first woman speechmaker in America to published author, surely I can obey the calling that the Lord has placed on my heart to speak up on behalf of the oppressed.

I write this chapter with trembling hands, because I can just *see* my reader wincing at the forceful language of the jeremiad. It seems almost un-American to some. And yet, as if the biblical example of prophetic speaking weren't enough, two quotes from James Baldwin come to mind.

The first comes from *Notes of a Native Son:* "I love America more than any other country in the world, and, exactly for that reason, I insist on the right to criticize her perpetually." The second comes from a 1969 interview with Dick Cavett in which he rightfully pointed out the double standard America has for her white patriots and Black activists. To paraphrase, when Patrick Henry says, "Give me liberty, or give me death," it's noble; when a Black man (or woman) says the same thing, it's frowned upon.

Make no mistake: we are called to a higher standard than patriotism. Our God has toppled nations more powerful than ours, and he will remain on his throne long after America's glory days are past. But to call the critique of America *un*patriotic—to call the dogged pursuit of liberty and justice for all surprising or radical—is to apply a double standard.

Our ragtag group of colonies rebelled against the most powerful nation in the world because of taxation without representation.

Our Black forefathers and foremothers were technically represented in Congress, thanks to the three-fifths clause, and yet were *still not given the rights of citizens.* Their numbers were used to bolster the cause of the South and protect the representation of slaveholding states, but they themselves were not seen as having the rights of the people who used those numbers to their advantage.

If that's not worth dumping a little tea into the harbor, I don't know what is.

And, more important, if it is not worth holding accountable those who claim to be the people of God to live out the standards set forth in his Word, then I don't know what is.

I want to be brave like Maria because I want to love God the way that Maria did—enough to advocate for those for whom he has called me to advocate. Enough to call to repentance those whom he has called me to call to repentance. Enough to use whatever resources I have to proclaim the truth of his Word to any issue my country is facing.

David Walker's Christian beliefs spurred him to activism. The Lord used Maria's conversion and David Walker to spur Maria to activism. And that domino effect is still rippling throughout history. May Maria spur you as she has spurred me.

A Refined Negro Woman

Lucy Craft Laney

There is plenty of work for all who have the proper conception of the teacher's office, who know that all men are brothers, God being their common father. But the educated Negro woman must teach the "Black Babies;" she must come forward and inspire our men and boys to make a successful onslaught upon sin, shame, and crime.

—Lucy Craft Laney

For most of my teaching career, I worked in predominately white schools. I'll share in the next chapter how that job has had its ups and downs, but suffice it to say, I felt called to that environment, but eventually, the unique challenges wore me down to the point of quitting. I loved my students, despite our disparate heritage. But there was nothing quite like the one year that I spent teaching at an inner-city school in Minneapolis's diverse Phillips neighborhood.

It was my first time standing in a classroom and staring out at a sea of faces that reflected my own heritage back to me. I felt a certain freedom in those rooms that hasn't been replicated since. Pregnant with my firstborn son for the bulk of that year, my normal fun-loving, laid-back teaching style took on a no-nonsense edge. More than one eighth-grade boy remarked, "Dang, Mrs. Holmes. You sound like my mama."

Even though most of the students we served were minorities, most of the faculty were white. For many of the students, my English class and my friend's Spanish class would be the only high school experiences they would have with Black teachers. And up until that point in my life, it had been my only experience teaching a majority-Black student body.

So when February rolled around, I decided to dedicate Black History Month to my favorite period in Black American history: the Harlem Renaissance.

My second-born son is named Langston, so it should come as no surprise that the Harlem Renaissance—Langston Hughes's heyday—has always mystified me. Part of the reason *The Autobiography of Malcolm X* resonated with me so much at age sixteen was because of the peek into Harlem's art scene. Zora Neale Hurston, Claude McKay, Nella Larsen, and a host of other Black artists launched into the North during the heart of the Great Migration, and when their pens hit paper, it was magic.

I enjoyed introducing every one of my classes—from my rowdy seventh- and eighth-graders to my "too cool for school" seniors—to the works of the Harlem Renaissance. Though the school was majority Black, the curriculum was sometimes glaringly white, and it was the first time they had learned a whole unit about people who looked like them. I hope it was an amazing experience for them—but I *know* it was an amazing experience for me.

As those young minds of the Harlem Renaissance migrated from the South to the North and started to make their mark on the world, their southern roots made a decisive impact on who they would become as individuals and as artists. And one woman cultivated those roots the same way that I hope I'm cultivating the roots of my own students. Her name was Lucy Craft Laney.

Humble Beginnings

Lucy Craft Laney founded the Haines Normal and Industrial Institute, at one time serving more than nine hundred students in Augusta, Georgia. Never marrying, Lucy would pour her life into the institute to such a degree that she never left—living on campus even after a group of her students arranged a house for her across the street. By the time she died in 1933, she would leave an indelible mark on Georgia education. Sara Griffith Stanley was a teacher at Haines for a season, and so was Mary McLeod Bethune. So intense was Lucy's devotion to her beloved school that she is buried near its first site, on Phillips Street.

Lucy was born in April of 1854 to David and Louisa Laney. David and Louisa were both born into slavery. David's master allowed him to earn money by working odd jobs in town—a rarity for enslavers of the day—and the young man eventually saved up enough to purchase his freedom. He married Louisa when she was only thirteen, after purchasing her freedom as well. Louisa would continue to work for the Campbells, who had enslaved her, even once free, and Lucy would credit her love of learning to the extensive library of the Campbells. David himself became a Presbyterian minister.

Lucy was the seventh-born of ten children. Though not all of them survived into adulthood, she nevertheless grew up in a house full of people.

The Campbells had taught Louisa to read, and she passed this love of reading on to Lucy, making sure that her daughter was afforded every educational opportunity that arose. When the American Missionary Association[1] arranged for a post-war school for emancipated Black children in Macon, Georgia, Lucy was one of their first students.

I love that Lucy's education was, in part, the result of other Black educators who went out of their way to go down south and pass the baton. Lucy picked it up and ran with it. After Atlanta University was founded in 1865, she was part of the first graduating class at the tender age of fifteen. Afterward, she attended the Normal Department for teacher training.

In 1883, when Lucy was twenty-nine, the Board of Missions for Freemen convinced her to start a school in Augusta. While Lucy had close ties to Congregationalists as well as the Presbyterians who ran the mission board, she would most often receive money and support from the Presbyterian church. Lucy rented a room for her very first school from Christ Presbyterian Church. She started with a mere five students, and by the end of the first year that number had jumped to seventy-five; by the end of the second year that number had jumped to two hundred.

> Every time Lucy pursued space for her school to grow, the Lord blessed her endeavors.

Much of Lucy's work as head of school was to raise money, which she saw as missions work. And every time Lucy pursued space for her school to grow, the Lord blessed her endeavors.

Once her student body of two hundred had outgrown Christ Presbyterian Church, a white undertaker offered her a two-story house on Calhoun Street. Realizing that they would soon outgrow the two-story house, Lucy went to the General Assembly of the Northern Presbyterian Church in Minneapolis to solicit funding.[2] Said one onlooker who watched

Lucy speak, "It was a novel sight to me. A young colored girl brought greetings from her people and besought our mission board for more schools."[3]

Mrs. F.E.H. Haines, president of the Women's Department in the Presbyterian Church USA, was particularly encouraging to Lucy, impressed by the young woman's passion for her students. Mrs. Haines would become a generous benefactor, and Lucy would, in fact, go on to name her school after her.

By 1913, Lucy had gathered enough funds to build a school on Gwinnett Street. She had thirty-four faculty and nine hundred students when she opened Haines Normal and Industrial Institute.

Lucy helmed the school through hell and high water—literally, in the case of the latter. Once, a flood cut the school off from the rest of the world for three days. Another time, there was an epidemic of malaria among her students. And a fire destroyed one of the dormitories.

Yet Lucy persisted in her cause, seemingly undaunted by every single calamity. And her work was sorely needed in Georgia. Sadie Iola Daniel, who wrote *Women Builders* while Lucy Craft Laney was still at the Haines Institute, cites,

> The state has more than six million Negroes with thirty-six and one half percent of illiteracy as compared with seven and eight-tenths percent of illiteracy among whites, although the Negro group comprises forty-five and one-tenth percent of the total population. Few of the Georgia cities have provided adequately for Negro education and rural school facilities for Negroes are still meager. A report of the Julius Rosenwald fund shows that Georgia ranks tenth in the number of rural school buildings aided by that foundation between 1913 and 1928. The State ranks forty-eighth in provision for public education and forty-seventh in public health work. Of the children who start school in Georgia, fifty per cent never complete the fourth grade. Thus, Haines Institute, an oasis of knowledge in a desert of ignorant, provides for the thirsty.[4]

The Great Debate

The debate of the day was over whether Black students would be better served by learning trades or learning liberal arts. Staunch commentators like Booker T. Washington maintained that the road to Black acceptance in white society was paved by respectability—and that respectability could be best achieved by a trade. Racial uplift, he argued, would be the result of hard work and elbow grease.

On the opposite end of the spectrum, others maintained the importance of a liberal arts education, arguing that the way to gain traction in society was through the ability to enter into meaningful intellectual discourse and to fight for equal rights regardless of respectability and trade.

Jennifer Lund Smith writes,

> Black educators at the turn of the century engaged in a fierce debate about the merits of a liberal arts education versus a vocational education. Booker T. Washington, the founder of Tuskegee Institute, articulated the argument that African Americans needed vocational skills above all, to gain economic power and independence. W.E.B. DuBois, who earned degrees at Fisk University and Harvard, and who taught economics and history at Atlanta University from 1897 to 1910, forcefully disagreed. He contended that intellectual parity would empower black Americans. In refusing to reject vocational education, Laney "mixed idealism and pragmatism." Furthermore, philanthropists tended to fund vocational schools, which they considered less threatening, more generously than liberal arts schools for black students, and the intense competition for benefactors' money most likely influenced Laney's decision to include vocational classes for her students.[5]

Lucy Craft Laney's school existed on the cusp of both of these ideals. Establishing her own curriculum, she offered both vocational *and* liberal arts education, satisfying both ends of the spectrum and gaining traction with her investors as well as her educational contemporaries. She attended Booker T. Washington's talks and was familiar with Tuskegee's pragmatic curriculum. It was obvious that she viewed it with respect. She taught practical skills that would transition well into the job market.

But she also taught them Latin. Laney had taught herself to read Latin at the tender age of twelve, translating Julius Caesar's *Commentaries on the Gallic War*.

I have taught Latin for six years out of my teaching career and I *might* be able to get through a paragraph of Caesar.

Lucy felt that teaching her students domestic arts and marketable skills was just as important as teaching them languages and humanities. She admonished her students to "stay in step with the progress of the world,"[6] seeming to borrow from DuBois's worldview.

In 1890, she added the first kindergarten in Augusta to her school. She would also go on to open Lamar Nursing School as an extension of Haines. Her graduates would go on to colleges such as Yale and Fisk.

> Lucy's school offered both vocational and liberal arts education, satisfying both ends of the spectrum.

Although a teacher first, Lucy was also involved in activism. In 1917, she hosted the organizational meeting of the Augusta chapter of the NAACP, helping to found the chapter in 1918.

According to the *New Georgia Encyclopedia*, "Haines not only offered its students a holistic approach to education but also served as a cultural center for the African American community. The school hosted orchestra concerts, lectures by nationally famous guests, and various social events."[7]

So impactful was Haines on the youth of Georgia that, along with Reverend Martin Luther King Jr. and Reverend Henry McNeal Turner, Lucy would be one of the first Black Americans to have their portraits hung in the Georgia State Capitol.

Now Lucy Craft Laney High School, Lucy's life's work, still lives on to this day. A museum stands in Augusta in her honor, detailing her contribution to the young people of the state.

Almost Too Famous to Be Forgotten

When I first started compiling a list of women's names for this book, Lucy Craft Laney felt almost too illustrious. A museum, a school, and other Augusta staples bear the honor of her name. Could she really be counted among the never known or the forgotten?

I decided to include her, though, because Lucy Craft Laney was never a name I knew. And if I had heard her name, I'm not sure I ever understood what a staunchly Christian woman she was, or how big a part the Presbyterian church played in her ability to found and run her school.

It was, in fact, Presbyterian Marjorie E. W. Smith who remarked in 1934 that Lucy had been "staunchly Christian,"[8] and Lucy brought those values to bear in every aspect of educating her young charges. Reverend Dr. E. P. Cowan, secretary of the Freedmen's Board of the Presbyterian Church, said that Lucy's father, David Laney, "has put no son into the Gospel ministry to succeed him, but his worthy daughter, Lucy, is today practically doing the work of a faithful minister and servant of Christ. Miss Laney is a graduate of Atlanta University and has an education of which no woman in this land, white or colored, need be ashamed."[9]

Similar to Nannie Helen Burroughs and the male counterpart she was often compared to (Washington), Lucy Craft Laney also believed that respectability and hard work could gain her young charges respect in the eyes of the white communities they were entering.[10]

When I think of Lucy—the daughter of two once-enslaved people, who watched her hard work and intellect open doors that had been closed to her ancestors for many years—I understand this perspective. The young woman found herself on the cusp of Black citizenship during a time in America's history when her kinsmen were wrestling with what it meant to be part of American society. Cast into a new era of the fight for equality, education had always been a key in Lucy's life—first for her father in his quest to purchase his own freedom, then for her own mother in her unique position as a literate enslaved woman, and then for Lucy herself, as a young graduate and professional.

Lucy's road to agency was paved with books. She walked that road and guided many others along it. Notably, her own school was first intended to be a school for girls, but when young men came to her door, she couldn't bear to send them away.

Excellence and Femininity

In many ways, Lucy was not a picture of nineteenth-century femininity. She was a Black woman, unmarried, who wore her hair cropped close. And yet, Lucy prized both femininity and motherhood and saw them as valuable tools in the fight for racial uplift. In 1899, she addressed the Hampton Negro Conference about the need for more teachers—and her desire for more Black teachers.

> If the educated colored woman has a burden, and we believe she has—what is that burden? How can it be lightened, how may it be lifted? What it is can be readily seen perhaps better than told, for it constantly annoys to irritation; it bulges out as did the load of Bunyan's Christian ignorance with its inseparable companions, shame and crime and prejudice.[11]

Lucy continues,

Women are by nature fitted for teaching very young children; their maternal instinct makes them patient and sympathetic with their charges. Negro women of culture, as kindergartners and primary teachers have a rare opportunity to lend a hand to the lifting of these burdens, for here they may instill lessons of cleanliness, truthfulness, loving kindness, love for nature, and love for Nature's God. Here they may daily start aright hundreds of our children; here, too, they may save years of time in the education of the child; and may save many lives from shame and crime by applying the law of prevention. In the kindergarten and primary school is the salvation of the race. For children of both sexes from six to fifteen years of age, women are more successful as teachers than men. This fact is proven by their employment.[12]

As much as we may be tempted to squabble about traditional roles of women in society (and we are allowed to squabble with these women, no matter how illustrious their careers or how great their love of God may have been), what resonates with me most is Lucy's clear desire for Black educators to take on a role that she deems supremely important in the battle for equality.

We know that public school teachers are less ethnically diverse than their students[13]—having worked in private schools for the vast majority of my teaching career, I know those numbers are even bleaker. Granted, I teach mostly white students, and Lucy was specifically seeking to cultivate the minds of Black pupils. Nevertheless, regardless of the color of the sea of young faces looking back at me, I might have been the only Black female authority figure they would encounter during their education.

Laney's school existed before school integration would cause innumerable private schools to pop up all over the southern states. She existed in a world where Black education was a new and burgeoning phenomenon, one she was a beneficiary of as her education was helmed by women like Sara G. Stanley and Charlotte Forten Grimké at the close of the Civil War. She was on the front lines of cultivating what it meant not only to be Black and educated, but a Black educator who was pouring herself into the next generation.

In one generation, Black Americans went from a largely enslaved caste to being active citizens of the country that had enslaved them. We had to overcome generations of legislated illiteracy, not just at the most basic level, but in hopes of participating in the marketplace of ideas and being taken seriously in spite of the color of our skin. We've already talked about striving to understand where Nannie Helen Burroughs's taste for respectability came from, and it is not difficult to extend that same grace to Laney.

Not only was Black education changing—education as a whole in America was morphing.

> In one of the great changes that occurred after the Civil War, southerners, both black and white, redefined the meaning of education in the South. Southern states had not created public educational systems during the antebellum period; hence, possession of an education was reserved for the elite who could afford tutors and private schools. In the antebellum—and postbellum—South education signified power. After the war, however, the freedpeople made education a priority and essentially forced the issue of public education, for children of all races and all classes.[14]

Talking Less—Doing More

As much as Lucy Craft Laney meant to so many, records of her speeches are scarce. I love that about her, though. She seemed to be a woman more focused on *doing* than on talking, speaking only when necessary—to garner funds for her school, to try to recruit more Black teachers, and of course, in the classroom. She seemed to be a quiet, no-nonsense woman, which makes her impact on her pupils that much more extraordinary.

It was clear from other speeches Lucy gave that she prized the institution of the Black family—particularly that of motherhood. In a speech given at the Atlanta University Conference on Negro Problems (arranged by W.E.B. DuBois) in 1898, she stated,

> Motherhood, honored by our blessed Master, is the crown of womanhood. This gives her not only interest in the home and society, but also authority. She should be interested in the welfare of her own neighbors' children. To women has been committed the responsibility of making the laws of society, making environments for children.[15]

It is also clear that her idea of motherhood was not limited to the keeping of the home (skills she proudly taught in her school) but extended to the shaping of a woman's mind, and concern not only for her own children but for her neighbors' children. Mothers were not an island unto themselves, meant only to influence the goings-on of their own homes, but rather, a connection between their own children and concerns to the children and concerns of others within their societies and environments.

And Lucy presided over the school with the dedication of a mother.

> If the building has been cold, she herself has found what ailed the furnace. If some girl who was supposed to be working in the kitchen needed to get out-of-doors in the sunshine, Miss Laney would take her place, bake the bread, peel the potatoes, or wash pots and pans. When some exceptionally good movie comes to town, she sees to it that all the children enjoy it. The salutatorian of the 1930 graduating class tells how Miss Laney

took her younger sister to her home and put her in her own bed
in order that she might keep her warm.[16]

She once left an interview early to help one of her young
students finish building a dollhouse.[17]

Lucy was known by everyone who had the pleasure of inter-
acting with her as a tenderhearted woman who was not afraid
to give of herself, not just to the cause of education, but to the
service of the children whom she dearly loved. As a mother
myself, I can only hope my children will say the same of my
contribution to our household; I can only hope that my students
got to see a glimpse of Lucy Craft Laney's service in me during
my years as a teacher.

The Legacy of Lucy Laney

When she died, the *Augusta Chronicle* described her home-
going as "more like a coronation than a funeral."[18] An estimated
five thousand people attended the funeral, each one a testament
to Lucy Craft Laney's impact on the lives of her students and
beyond. Her quest to build up a culture of Black excellence and
education was well accomplished.

From the age of fourteen, Lucy Craft Laney knew what she
wanted to be: a teacher. And she spent her entire life in dogged
pursuit of this goal. Her focus was on the uplift of the Black
youth of Augusta, Georgia, and she threw herself so completely
into that focus that she lived on the campus where she taught.
She operated within her small corner of the world with a faithfulness that we would do well to emulate, even if our different
corners seem further reaching than hers.

Lucy is a testament to what it looks like to faithfully stick
to a task. Although she was involved in activism as well as
education, the bulk of her time was spent in the classroom and
in facilitating the classroom experiences of other teachers. She

does not have a host of speeches that I can pull from to illustrate her faith in Christ, but perhaps more than any other woman in this book, she has the testimony of the people who knew her and saw her service up close.

I do not know if there will be five thousand people at my funeral, or if I will live to a ripe old age as Miss Lucy Laney did. I do not know what the testimony of my life will be when all is said and done. There are so many different parts of me at play—believer, wife, mother, teacher, writer—and, depending on the season, different descriptives may rise to the top. But I hope that whatever my priorities are as each day goes by, I am known for the fullhearted service that Lucy was known for. For advocacy that was not for an audience but was lived out, day by day, in a classroom full of perhaps thankless children. For teaching people who would go further and do more than she could ever dream, thereby multiplying her influence by the thousands.

What an incredible testimony of God's faithfulness this woman was. From enslaved parentage to a thorough education lived out in quiet, humble intellect and service to others. What a legacy she left, not only for her students, but for every person who picks up her story.

What a legacy she has left me.

What a legacy she has left you.

9

Daughter of a Legacy
Charlotte Forten Grimké

I shall dwell again among "mine own people." I shall gather my scholars about me, and see smiles of greeting break over their dusky faces. My heart sings a song of thanksgiving, at the thought that even I am permitted to do something for a long-abused race.

—Charlotte Forten Grimké

It is hard to be a building block in a family legacy.

I know it from experience.

Forging my own path while respecting and appreciating the path my parents set before me is a constant balancing act. Brimming with gratitude for all that my parents were and are for me—did and do for me—while seeking growth and healing from their mistakes and oversights is tricky in a world that likes to court scandal. I talk about my parents in therapy a bit more than the average person *because* of the gigantic, looming presence they are in my life. Not only am I the daughter of a (in some circles) well-known pastor, I'm a homeschool graduate who did not leave the nest until I married my husband at the age of twenty-four.

For better or for worse, my world was really small until I left my home. My larger-than-life dad, my poster child of a homeschool mom, and my eight younger siblings were my *life*—job and grad school notwithstanding. Entering marriage plunged me into a whole new world of figuring out who *I* was as I tied my life to another person's. No longer were my decisions merely an appendage that felt pressured to move along with the powerful current of my countercultural family. Even though many people still *saw* them that way, the reality was, I was a Holmes now. And it was only as a Holmes—invested in a one-flesh union with my husband—that I realized that I am an individual.

My journey toward separating my idea of self from my family of origin is difficult and ongoing. But when I think about the life of Charlotte Forten Grimké—daughter, granddaughter, and niece of abolitionists, activists, entrepreneurs, teachers, and world changers—my journey suddenly seems simpler. Rather than waiting for marriage to move boldly into her life's ambition (as I did, and as was common with the women of her day), Charlotte did not marry until the age of forty-one. By that time, she had spent years as a teacher, folklorist, and prolific diarist.

Charlotte did not accomplish her life's mission by bucking against her family of origin's calling, nor did she accomplish it by following in lockstep with the path that had been set before her. Instead, she used the legacy she had inherited to galvanize her to action on behalf of the people that her family spent their lives serving.

The Beginning of a Legacy

Charlotte's legacy begins with her great-great-grandfather, who was brought over from West Africa as a slave in the 1680s.[1] As soon as he was able, he purchased his freedom and devoted his life to learning a trade. His son, Thomas, would die shortly after the birth of James Forten, Charlotte's grandfather. James's mother made sure he received an education, and he attended a school funded by famed Quaker abolitionist Anthony Benezet.[2] At the age of fourteen, James would join the Revolutionary War effort, and upon the war's end, after a short stint traveling in England, he would become an apprentice to sailmaker Robert Bridges. Through sail-making, Forten would eventually become a businessman.[3]

James Forten would leverage his family business by inventing an instrument that made his sail-making even more proficient, and he became one of the wealthiest Black men in Pennsylvania as a result. In addition to his business sense, James was an active abolitionist, providing early funding for William Lloyd Garrison's magazine, *The Liberator*, co-founding the Free African Society, and applying his voice to the same jeremiad tradition as his contemporary David Walker. He often drew upon the patriotism of his fellow servicemen to defend his personhood as a Black man: "We hold this truth to be self-evident, that GOD created all men equal, and is one of the most prominent features in the Declaration of Independence, and in that glorious fabric of collected wisdom, our noble Constitution."[4]

Like Elizabeth Freeman before him, Forten asserted that the founding documents of the country where he resided—the country that he had fought for—applied to its Black residents.

He stated these thoughts in *Letters from a Man of Colour*, which he self-published in 1813 on the precipice of proposed legislation that, if passed, would prevent Black people from migrating to Pennsylvania. The legislature had passed an Act for the Gradual Abolition of Slavery in 1780, and Pennsylvanians were nervous at the prospect of having more free Black people among them. James was poised to make a case for his humanity in light of that fear.

In addition to pouring himself into the important work of abolition for the enslaved population, he worked incredibly hard to serve the free population. He started a school with Grace Douglass (mother of the last woman in this collection, Sarah Mapps Douglass) that served free Black students—some of whom were James's own children.

James and his wife, also name Charlotte, would have six children. Sarah Louise would become a poet, abolitionist, and frequent author for *The Liberator*. Harriet would help found the Philadelphia Female Anti-Slavery Society and do important work as a suffragette. Margaretta, the aunt closest to Charlotte, would become an abolitionist, an educator, and a poet. And Robert Bridges, Charlotte's father, would become a businessman, mathematician, orator, and inventor. One of his inventions—a novel telescope—would be displayed at Philadelphia's Franklin Institute.

Charlotte's mother died when she was a young girl, and Robert delegated her care to his mother and his sister Margaretta. Robert himself moved to Canada, frustrated with the racism he frequently encountered in the States. He would not return until the dawn of the Civil War, enlisting in the 43rd US Colored Troops Infantry regiment at the age of fifty.

Charlotte held a deep esteem for her father, writing in her journal,

> I thank father very much for his kindness, and am determined that so far as I am concerned, he shall never have cause to regret it. I will spare no effort to become what he desires that I should be; to prepare myself well for the responsible duties of

a teacher, and to live for the good that I can do my oppressed and suffering fellow creatures.[5]

She saw him as an example of the kind of activism she hoped to accomplish later in life, and she did her father proud.

Another Educated Homeschooler

Charlotte's own education began at home. Raised in Philadelphia's elite Black community, she was privately educated. Like me, Charlotte was technically a homeschool graduate, but she far surpassed me, teaching herself French, German, and Latin while at home. She would go on to attend Salem Normal School for teaching in 1856, becoming Salem's first Black graduate and the first Black woman to teach in white classrooms in the state of Massachusetts.

As a Black teacher who worked in predominately white spaces for most of my ten years of educational experience, I know that the bravery and poise Charlotte had to exhibit in her classrooms cannot be overstated.

Throughout my years of teaching in white classrooms, I had a host of awkward encounters, from the innocuous "What's on your head?" when I tied my hair in a scarf to the slightly more offensive "Well, of *course* you care about racism. You're Black. Why would I care as much as you care?"

One experience in particular stands out to me. Though I was an English major, in recent years my love for history has taken center stage in both my teaching and my writing endeavors. Anyone who teaches with me knows that I have a particular affinity for the Civil War and its innumerable causes. One day, another teacher was getting ready to have a class discussion about the founding fathers' attitudes toward slavery and she came to me for some advice. I was poised to give her resources, but in a comedy of errors, I ended up standing in front of a class full of white kids, completely unprepared for the ensuing discussion. The fact that it appeared that the only Black teacher on campus had been thrust in front of them to talk about slavery was awkward in and of itself, but the awkwardness was further exacerbated by what I perceived as a marked lack of empathy toward enslaved human beings on our soil.

I went to my car and cried afterward, frustrated that I hadn't had time to gather source documents and rally my answers to statements like "No one knew slavery was wrong back then," "Some slaves were just really happy living with their masters," and "What were they even supposed to do if they got free?" I called my husband and told him that standing there felt like defending my own humanity to a room full of apathetic teenagers. Questions that were innocuous to them felt very personal for me.

I was able to redo the lecture with different results. Apologies were made, misunderstandings set to rights, miscommunications properly communicated. I survived.

What I *cannot begin to imagine* is being a Black teacher in the 1860s teaching children whose only notions of Black people were of a subservient caste in the society that they were blessed to occupy. In spite of the fact that Charlotte grew up in a privileged upper-class household, she was still a Black woman living at a time when America was sharply divided in a system designed to subjugate its Black residents to such a degree that their very citizenship was often questioned. Even in a progressive town like Salem, Charlotte's presence as a woman of color was a staggering statement.

Much like Frances Ellen Watkins Harper, Charlotte Grimké was keenly aware of how tenuous freedom was for many other Black people on American soil. On May 25, 1854, she wrote,

Did not intend to write this evening, but have just heard of something that is worth recording;—something which must ever rouse in the mind of every true friend of liberty and humanity, feelings of the deepest indignation and sorrow.

Another fugitive from bondage has been arrested; a poor man, who for two short months has trod the soil and breathed the air of the "Old Bay State," was arrested like a criminal in the streets of her capital, and is now kept strictly guarded,—a double police force is required, the military are in readiness; and all this done to prevent a man, whom God has created in his own image, from regaining that freedom which he, in common with every human being, is endowed. I can only hope and pray most earnestly that Boston will not again disgrace herself by sending him back to a bondage worse than death; or rather that she will redeem herself from the disgrace which his arrest alone has brought upon her.[6]

Charlotte's journal is, in and of itself, a marvel. Kept from 1854 to 1892, it records Charlotte's life from her perspective—the things that were important to her, the things that enraged her, the things that discouraged her, the things that gave her joy, the things that struck her passion. There is an intimacy in reading a journal that is quite unlike any other type of account—even an autobiography is an edited account meant for public consumption. But a journal offers us a unique look into the personality of this dynamic woman.

> Charlotte was keenly aware of how tenuous freedom was for many other Black people on American soil.

The journal also attests to her thorough education. She read one hundred books in a year as a teenager and she records her thoughts about many of the texts she read. The first entry in her diary is about Dickens's *Hard Times*, which I read around the same age. She quotes William Cowper, Elizabeth Barrett Browning, and others.

But not only is the journal a testament to Charlotte's thorough education, it is also a testament to her passionate distaste for slavery. Several entries mention her hope of emancipation, her disgust with pastors' seeming approval of the institution, and her desire to be involved in anti-slavery work. She very closely follows the case of Anthony Burns, the runaway mentioned in the above entry, and expresses her intense disappointment in her country when he is sentenced back to slavery:

> Today Massachusetts has again been disgraced; again she has showed her submission to the Slave Power; and Oh! With what deep sorrow do we think of what will doubtless be the fate of that poor man, when he is again consigned to the hours of slavery. With what scorn must that government be regarded which cowardly assembles thousands of soldiers to satisfy the demands of slaveholders; to deprive of his freedom a man, created in God's own image, whose sole offense is the color of his skin! And if resistance is offered to this outrage, these soldiers are to shoot down American citizens without mercy; and this by express orders of a government which proudly boasts of being the freest in the world; this on the very soil where the Revolution of 1776 began; in sight of the battlefield, where thousands of brave men fought and died in opposing British tyranny, which was nothing compared with the American oppression of today.[7]

Like her grandfather before her, the young Charlotte saw the existence of slavery in the "land of the free" as an unforgivable contradiction. She would end up devoting a large chunk of her life to the education of the people she so desperately wanted to see set free.

Teaching the Contraband of War

The law that led to the capture of Anthony Burns is the same law that would lead to Charlotte's future in South Carolina.

In 1850, the Fugitive Slave Act became the latest in a string of compromises the federal government was making in order to appease the South's desire to keep slavery alive and well in the Union. As previously discussed, this law not only made it illegal for any northerner to aid and abet runaway enslaved people, it also compelled northerners who knew about fugitive slaves to work with slaveholders for their return. We've seen Frances Ellen Watkins Harper and others respond to the implications of this legislation.

After the Civil War began, though, the Fugitive Slave Act presented a bit of a conundrum for Union troops. Enslaved people who lived near enough to Union camps were breaking free and going to these camps for sanctuary. Under the Fugitive Slave Act, the Union soldiers were potentially breaking federal law by allowing the formerly enslaved to stay; however, as the South was in rebellion, they did not want to facilitate returning the southern labor force. And so the seeds of contraband camps were born.

> At the start of the war, the Union had no policy to deal with the African Americans seeking protection. Individual commanders made their own decisions. Some commanders put them to work for Union troops while others returned them to plantation owners. At Fort Monroe in Hampton, Virginia, Union Maj. General Benjamin Butler refused to send three fugitives back into the bonds of slavery. He classified the escaping slaves as contraband of war. This term meant that once the fleeing slaves crossed Union army lines, they were classified as property. All enemy property that fell into Union hands constituted contraband and would not be returned. Because of Butler's actions, a federal policy was instituted on August 6, 1861—fugitive slaves were declared to be 'contraband of war' if their labor had been used to aid the Confederacy in anyway. If found to be contraband, they were declared free.[8]

General Butler was not an abolitionist, and had, in fact, voted for Jefferson Davis in the past. However, he knew that withholding the runaways was a smart tactical move. It removed responsibility from the Union soldiers to abide by the Fugitive Slave Act, because the southern states' rebellion made that act null and void. Further, it played off the southern laws that dehumanized enslaved people by treating them as property: now that "property" was considered the spoils of war.

And so contraband camps began to crop up all over the Union-occupied South, particularly in Georgia and South Carolina. Black teachers began making their way south to aid in the camps, setting up schools for the formerly enslaved. These camps became the first experience of American citizenship for many a Black refugee from the South, and women like Mary S. Peake were there to welcome them and to strive to aid the transition.

In 1861, Charlotte Forten was recruited by the federal government to teach emancipated slaves on the Sea Islands of South Carolina.[9] The area had been abandoned by many white plantation owners when the Union arrived, leaving behind scores of newly freed Black people. The Sea Islands weren't a contraband camp, in the sense that the freed people there were not runaways, but served a similar purpose.

Charlotte the Folklorist

The culture of the Sea Islands was different from any place Charlotte had ever experienced. Many plantation owners allowed their enslaved laborers to live on the islands, while they themselves lived on the mainland to avoid diseases common in the area. As the majority of people who actually inhabited the area were Black and largely self-sustaining, Charlotte was stepping into an entirely new culture.

The culture shock was real. Often discouraged by the language barrier between herself and her students (the Sea Islands had their own dialect) and the customs that were completely foreign to her, Charlotte also battled with health issues there that would follow her for the rest of her life. Yet even as she struggled to serve the inhabitants of the islands well, she played an important part in capturing their culture and history for the rest of the watching country, becoming the very first folklorist to do so.

She would share her observations in the May 1864 edition of the *Atlantic Monthly*. Her narrative would bring attention to the thousands of newly freed Black people whose stories might not otherwise have been told.

Many of the grown people are desirous of learning to read. It is wonderful how a people who have been so long crushed to the earth, so imbruted as these have been,—and they are said to be among the most degraded negroes of the South,—can have so great a desire for knowledge, and such a capability for attaining it. One cannot believe that the haughty Anglo-Saxon race, after centuries of such an experience as these people have had, would be very much superior to them. And one's indignation increases against those who, North as well as South, taunt the colored race with inferiority while they themselves use every means in their power to crush and degrade them, denying them every right and privilege, closing against them every avenue of elevation and improvement. Were they, under such circumstances, intellectual and refined, they would certainly be vastly superior to any other race that ever existed."[10]

She especially enjoyed sharing their hymns:

> Go down in de Lonesome Valley; My brudder, you
>   waut to git religion,
> Go down in de Lonesome Valley.
>
> CHORUS.
>
> "Go down in de Lonesome Valley,
> Go down in de Lonesome Valley, my Lord,
> Go down in de Lonesome Valley,
> To meet my Jesus dere!

"Oh, feed on milk and honey,
Oh, feed on milk and honey, my Lord,
Oh, feed on milk and honey,
Meet my Jesus dere!

Oh, John he brought a letter,
Oh, John he brought a letter, my Lord,
Oh, Mary and Marta read 'em
Meet my Jesus dere!

CHORUS.

"Go down in de Lonesome Valley," etc.[11]

She painted a picture of a principled, deeply religious people whom she was blessed to serve, in spite of the culture shock she often experienced in their service. In Charlotte's diary, we have a unique account of the day-to-day trials and triumphs of ministering in another culture. The picture painted isn't always a rosy one—at times, the reader may recoil from the apparent pride with which she held her customs in comparison to the customs of the people she was serving. But the theme Charlotte returned to was the inherent dignity of the formerly enslaved people whom she taught.

She spoke with devotion of mothers who came to her class with babies on their hips, ready to *finally* learn how to read—of grandmothers who sat learning next to their grandchildren. She spoke of their deep, spiritual convictions and their church traditions. She spoke of her calling to serve, not just as a teacher for reading, writing, and arithmetic, but for Sunday school and hymn singing as well. Charlotte poured herself into the inhabitants of the Sea Islands, even when her own health limitations got in the way.

Charlotte would spend her life trying to right the wrongs she witnessed as a young girl.

Mrs. Charlotte Forten Grimké

Charlotte Forten would not become Charlotte Forten Grimké for several more years. After leaving the Sea Islands, she continued to teach, first in Boston again, and later in DC. At forty-one, she would marry Presbyterian minister Francis Grimké, who had an impressive pedigree of his own (nephew of the famed abolitionist Grimké sisters). Francis was the son of a slaveholder and an enslaved woman, and his aunts would help him to get an education, first at Lincoln University in Pennsylvania. Francis would go from Lincoln to Howard, where he studied law until he felt that God was calling him to ministry. He would graduate from Princeton Theological Seminary in 1878.

> The theme Charlotte returned to was the inherent dignity of the formerly enslaved people whom she taught.

The Grimkés would have one child together, but that child would die in infancy.

Charlotte and Francis devoted the rest of their lives to the spreading of the Gospel and the reconciliatory love of Christ Jesus. Charlotte married a man whose boldness in the cause of justice matched every bit of the boldness in her pedigree, and she married a man whose love for the Bride of Christ matched and exceeded that boldness.

In advice to fellow preachers that still rings true today, Reverend Grimké said,

> Help us, O Lord, more and more, as thy servants, to realize that in and of ourselves we can do nothing: we are only instruments in thy hand, and our effectiveness as instruments depends entirely upon whether or whether not the Spirit uses us. From beginning to end, all effective work is due to the presence and power of the Spirit in the preacher and in the people to whom he

speaks. The more fully we understand this, and the more fully, after we have made the most careful preparation, we depend upon the Spirit in all that we do or attempt to do, the more certain we may be of results.[12]

It is in this Spirit-led humility that the Grimkés continued their service to the body of Christ throughout the rest of their lives.

Charlotte would continue to write, publishing some of her poems later in life. She would go on to help found the National Association of Colored Women. She and Francis would serve DC's Fifteenth Street Presbyterian Church. By the time Charlotte died in 1914, she had lived a life full of advocacy for others.

A Legacy That Lives On

As I have written this book, I have pondered the unique legacies of these ten women. Of the ten of them, only a couple had children who survived infancy and only some had husbands they were blessed to be married to for most of their lives. They are widows, single women who never married, or mothers who buried their children far too soon. And in this way, it can be difficult to see a lasting legacy—especially in the sense of the Forten family dynasty from which Charlotte hailed.

I grew up being taught a message of multigenerational faithfulness that prizes family legacy and family line. At this writing, I have given birth to not one but two sons who will carry on the Holmes family name, and I hope they do it with half as much dignity as the Forten clan did theirs. We have a Bible chock full of genealogies that show us the importance of family lines, right?

Well, yes and no. Yes, the Bible is full of genealogies. And yes, those family lines are incredibly important. But they aren't important because flesh-and-blood legacy reigns supreme; they are important because Christ reigns supreme. Following the seed of the woman (Genesis 3:16) from Eve all the way down to Mary isn't an exercise in genetic purity or family fame but rather an exercise in faithfulness. God promised in the very beginning that he would send his son to take on the sins of the world, and he kept that promise through generations of childbearing that culminated in the bearing of the Son of God.

That Son of God, Jesus Christ, then turned to his disciples and reminded them that the most important thing we have to give the world isn't our temporal family legacy, but our eternal one. In fact, he told the disciples that if their family didn't understand their commitment to him—if family stood in the way of their obedience to him—then that family needed to be forsaken (Mathew 19:29).

This understanding offers us a radical departure from a culture that used to prize sons over daughters because of the preservation of a family name. We have a family name that is above every other name in the person and work of Christ Jesus.

The Fortens were an amazing family. God used them in truly phenomenal ways, and he gave them a legacy that any inheritor could be proud of. Yet that legacy did not end with Charlotte any more than it ended with the never-married Margaretta. That legacy doesn't just belong to the Fortens, but to anyone who proclaims the name of Christ and obeys him even when it is not politically or socially expedient to do so.

This book boasts of mothers who never bore children; of members of the Bride of Christ who never wore wedding rings; of family legacies written not in genealogies, but in the history of the faithful God they served. And while an entirely new book could be written about the women who served God in traditional family structures where they married young and faithfully raised a passel of children, these ten women offer us a less-heard story of feminine strength and courage.

I do not have a family tree that looks like the Fortens', but I know what it is to be raised by faithful parents. I know what it is to become an adult and grapple with what faithfulness looks like for me, and for my children. But even if my sons never marry and never bear another Holmes, the legacy I hope to leave them isn't about the Holmeses' greatness—our obedience—our excellence—but rather, about the same God whom Charlotte and Francis served.

This is the only family legacy that will last.

10

She Leaned upon the Rock of Ages

Sarah Mapps Douglass

I know from blessed, heart-cheering experience the excellency of having a God to trust to in seasons of trial and conflict. . . . What but this can uphold our fainting footsteps in the swellings of Jordan? It is the only thing worth living for—the only thing that can disarm death of his sting. I am earnestly solicitous that each of us may adopt this language: I have no hope in man, but much in God—Much in the rock of ages."

—Sarah Mapps Douglass

I did not start to learn about the pivotal role Black Christians had played in Christian history until I became Presbyterian.

That is not to say that the only Black heroes and heroines of the faith are Presbyterian. In this book alone, we have a collection of Baptists, Methodists, and, in Sarah Mapps Douglass, a Quaker. As a woman who grew up Baptist, there are so many more Baptist examples I could have cited—Dr. Lulu Fleming, Naomi Crawford, Lucy Ann Henry Cole, Nora A. Gordon, Clara Howard, and others. George Leile was the first Black American to be ordained in the Baptist church, and the first Baptist missionary to go abroad.

But it was through my newly sprouted Presbyterian roots that I first began to discover people like Francis and Charlotte Forten Grimké, Maria Fearing, Alonzo and Althea Brown Edmiston, Sara G. Stanley, Betsey Stockton, and Lucy Craft Laney. The Presbyterian Church was the driving donor of the American Missionary Association, instrumental in sending teachers and founding schools for the newly emancipated in the wake of the Civil War.

More than any other denomination, Presbyterians sprouted up in my research as those most willing to send Black missionaries, ordain Black ministers, and educate Black parishioners. But, of course, my eyes are especially peeled for Presbyterian influences as a new and enthusiastic addition to the Presbyterian Church of America.

Other denominations, too, felt the importance of taking a stand on the issue of slavery.

> The intense feeling which arose over the slavery issue brought about a separation within the ranks of Methodism in 1844. This was followed by the cleavage of the Baptists in 1845, of the New School Presbyterians and Methodist Protestants in 1858, of the Old School Presbyterians, of the Protestant Episcopalians in 1861, and of the Lutherans in 1863.[1]

Yet by the time Methodist, Baptists, Presbyterians, Episcopalians, and Lutherans began wrestling with these issues, the Society of Friends had long established a history of taking a stand on slavery.

Quakers were questioning slavery's morality in states like North Carolina as early as the 1770s. In fact, though a 1741 law in the state forbade the emancipation of slaves by private citizens, Thomas Newby and ten other Quakers freed forty enslaved Black people in direct violation of this law in 1776,[2] sparking a string of petitions from Quaker residents of North Carolina to outlaw slavery in the state.[3] Quakers in North Carolina became so creative in their efforts to emancipate enslaved Black people that they were outlawed from purchasing them.

In the face of the many Protestants—both preachers and laypeople—who were complicit in America's participation in the horror that is chattel slavery, it can be easy to elevate the Quakers to hero status, wondering why more religious white Americans couldn't follow in their illustrious footsteps. And indeed, we have much to learn from the Society of Friends when it comes to consistency in rightly applying the Word of God with our brothers and sisters in Christ.

However, one woman—Sarah Mapps Douglass—took on even the Society for its inconsistency with applying the brotherhood of all men. And in typical Sarah Mapps Douglass fashion, she was fearless in her pursuit of justice.

Philadelphia Royalty

Sarah Mapps Douglass was born in 1806 in Philadelphia, Pennsylvania. Her parents were renowned abolitionists Robert Douglass Sr. and Grace Bustill Douglass—the latter of whom started a school for Black children with Charlotte Forten Grimké's father, James.

Grace's father, Cyrus Bustill (1732–1806) was the first in their family to become a Quaker. His Quaker master freed him after seven years of faithful service, then taught him the breadmaking trade. Cyrus sold bread throughout the Revolutionary War, making a comfortable life for his family.

He always championed the cause of freedom and gave of his means to promote it. He "would not perpetuate a race of slaves"; so he did not marry early in life. Finally he married Elizabeth Morey, daughter of Satterthwait, an Indian maiden of the Delaware tribe, who lived on the banks of the nigh river bearing their name, and with whom William Penn made his famous treaty for "Penn's Woods." She was as free as himself, and both were familiar with the manners and customs of the Friends.[4]

Like the Grimkés, the Douglasses were part of Philadelphia's Black elite. Robert Douglass Sr.'s family had emigrated from St. Kitts, and Robert himself was an officer of the Pennsylvania Augustine Society for the Education of People of Colour, which worked against the deportation and repatriation of Black Americans to Africa. In addition to her work as a teacher, Grace Bustill Douglass was an outspoken abolitionist in her own right.

Sarah was educated by a private tutor and grew up to become a teacher, first in New York, and later in Philadelphia.

In Philadelphia, Sarah would organize her own school for girls on Seventh Street. She would also serve as supervisor at the Institute for Colored Youth. In addition to shaping the minds of her students, Sarah was tireless in her efforts to further her own education. She helped organize the Philadelphia Female Literary Association for free Black women, which was founded in September of 1831. "Weekly meetings were devoted to reading and recitation, for the purpose of 'mental cultivation.'"[5] She would receive medical training from the Female Medical College of Pennsylvania as well as Pennsylvania Medical University.

In addition to these lettered accomplishments, Sarah Mapps Douglass would also be the first known signed Black female painter.[6]

Her work is often flowers painted at the top of her correspondence. These epistolary paintings are a subtle but distinct—and I argue radical—form of "creating back" to the stereotypes of her era. Douglass engages in a tradition of floriography in the sense that the depiction of flowers are a Victorian symbology in multiple ways. Not only is it a language of the upper class, but also of a delicacy and femininity that Black women were barred from.[7]

In this way, Sarah was similar to her brother Robert, himself an accomplished artist. His piece, *President George Washington Crossing the Delaware* was displayed in Independence Hall in 1832. Another piece, *Portrait of a Gentleman*, was included in the annual exhibition of the Pennsylvania Academy of the Fine Arts. "However, he was prevented from getting into the Academy to view his own work because of his race."[8]

All three of the Douglass children—Sarah, Robert, and William—would have full and enriching careers, but as a female teacher and abolitionist, Sarah's is the story that leaps from the page.

A Renaissance Woman

One of the most dynamic parts about Sarah Mapps Douglass is the fact that it seems like there was nothing this woman could not do. The word *Renaissance* springs to mind as I study the life of this ridiculously intelligent, accomplished, and classically educated Black woman.

Classical education is a big part of my life.

It all started with my own education. Around middle school, my parents made the shift to classical pedagogy—that is, a mode of education that is built around the classic languages and texts that have shaped Western thought. I quickly developed

> It seems like there was nothing this woman could not do. The word **Renaissance** springs to mind.

a deep love for all things ancient Grecian literature. I could tell you every Greek god or goddess, regale you with the history of each major Greek philosopher, even read and write a bit of Koine Greek. At thirty, some of the particulars of my Greek mythology and history obsession have faded, but I still reread *The Iliad* and *The Odyssey* every couple of years and jump at every opportunity to teach them. I have every translation of the works that I can find, and I enjoy comparing and contrasting them just for kicks and giggles.

My homeschooled nerdiness aside, it's often difficult to find other Black women who share my very niche interest in the foundations of Western culture. For better or for worse, the modern educational system doesn't put much stock in hammering out every nuance of ancient Greek thought. Allusions to Icarus, Narcissus, or even Odysseus and his sirens fly right over the heads of most of the peers outside of my little classical subculture, Black or white.

Imagine, then, my excitement on meeting a woman who was not only clearly classically educated herself, but who grew up to become an educator and Renaissance woman who would change the world.

She was so conversant with the classics she chose a pen name that reflected her love of them—a name she used to write subversive abolitionist texts.

In 1832, Sarah Mapps Douglass, a Quaker educator from Philadelphia, contributed three essays to William Lloyd Garrison's abolitionist paper, the *Liberator*, under the pseudonym "Sophanisba" . . . a Carthaginian princess who drank poison rather than be taken captive and paraded in a Roman triumph through the streets of Rome. Douglass, the daughter of African American abolitionists Robert and Grace Bustill Douglass, admired the pride and courage of the ancient Carthaginian woman.[9]

Douglass also used a pen name during her tenure as a member of the Female Literary Association, in which she took part with Charlotte Forten Grimké's aunt Sarah.

> No membership roster survives for the Female Literary Association, but eight of its members have been identified, although, except for Sarah Forten and Sarah Mapps Douglass only by the pseudonyms under which they published. In addition to Forten, who used the pseudonyms Ada and Magawisca and Douglass, who used Ella and Sophanisba, other association members whose work appeared in the *Liberator* include Zillah, Bera, Woodby, Zoe, Beatrice, and Anna Elizabeth. All were involved in an extensive network of African American women and men who had dedicated themselves to social and moral reform. Sarah Forten (1814–84) was the daughter of James Forten (1766–1842), a sail maker who had become one of the city's wealthiest African Americans. Committed to radical abolitionism, Forten had sent Garrison fifty-four dollars as an advance payment for twenty-seven subscriptions to the *Liberator*.[10]

The fabulous Forten family were not Sarah Mapps Douglass's only illustrious abolitionist connections—nor her only connection to Charlotte Forten Grimké. She would become very close to the Grimké sisters, Angelina and Sarah, who paid for the education of their nephew, Francis James Grimké. And it was the Grimké sisters who would convince Sarah to speak up about the hidden prejudices within the Society of Friends.

Quaker Accountability

Sarah had grown up as a Quaker—as many a Bustill before her—and her witnessing of the discrimination within the Society was one of her first memories. She watched as her mother was asked to sit apart from the rest of her Quaker brethren at meetings. As an adult, she recalled in a letter to a friend, "I remember well, wishing, (with the 'foolishness that is bound in the heart of child') that the meeting house would fall down, or that Friends would forbid our coming, thinking then that my mother would not persist among them."[11]

Sarah witnessed other slights and discriminations, from white Quakers not being allowed to sit with Black friends, to Black friends being separated from white friends even during funeral proceedings. She shared her frustrations with Angelina Grimké, who, with her permission, included them in an anonymously published pamphlet entitled "Society of Friends in the United States, Their Views of the Anti-Slavery Question, and Treatment of People of Color."

A Quaker refuted the claims of segregation during Quaker meetings, stating that "very few of them incline to attend our meetings. Friends' mode of worship does not suit their dispositions; they are fond of music and excitement, and hence they prefer their own meetings where they regularly hear singing and preaching."[12]

Sarah's response to the refutation signed simply "P.R." was published in *The National Anti-Slavery Standard*:

> In this, I think P. R. is mistaken. I have frequently heard my mother say that very many of our people inclined to Friends' mode of worship; she lamented the unchristian conduct that kept them out. I myself know some, whose hearts yearn for the quiet of your worshiping places, and who love the "still small voice" better than harp or viol. Some have gone out from "Friends" not because they prefer their own meetings, "where they regularly hear singing and preaching" but because they could not bear the cross of sitting on the "black bench." Ah, there are many poor stray starving sheep, wandering in this world's wilderness, who would gladly come into your green pastures, and repose them by your still waters; did not prejudice bar the entrance. I am persuaded the Lord has a

controversy with "friends" on this account. Let them see to it. S.M.D.[13]

You see, even though the Quakers were renowned for their exacting stance against slavery—outlawing their members from owning slaves, writing and petitioning constantly to see the blight of chattel slavery removed from the United States— some of them were still just as susceptible to prejudice as other Americans who surrounded them.

Undaunted Worship

Sarah's bravery here should not be missed. Discontent with the bare minimum of being in a congregation that agreed that slavery was anti-Christian and anti-Gospel, she wanted her Quaker brethren to take the next step: to believe that Black people were made in the image of God, and were endowed with dignity and significance because of this.

I have never been asked to sit in a segregated part of a church. I cannot imagine the shame Sarah must have felt on behalf of her mother, her friends, and herself when met with such a request. But I have failed to bring up more casual instances of racism[14] to my Christian brethren for fear of being met with a P. R.-level response again: "Our church is extremely welcoming to Black people. It's not *our* fault they don't want to come. They just like different music and different preaching styles."

It couldn't *possibly* be because the church is *un*welcoming to its Black visitors. No! It *must* be because Black people just don't want to be there. It couldn't be because we are allowing our cultural assumptions to color how we welcome visitors from different backgrounds.

Notably, Sarah did not let the prejudice within a few Quaker congregations keep her from worshiping. She found an assembly that welcomed her, and she pursued her commitment to God there.

> Then sweet voices sang a sweeter hymn, but while those notes of glorious music were ringing in my ear, my ears acknowledged the superior eloquence of silence—the beauty of sitting down in humility and heart-brokenness to wait the operation of the holy spirit—and then to feel its gentle influence distilling like dew upon my soul, and subduing every unholy wandering thought.[15]

The End of a Full Life

Much of Sarah's relationship with the Quaker church has been lost to history, due to the fact that she asked her family to destroy all of her correspondence after her death. The few samples that remain paint a picture of a woman who still prized the beauty of her religion in spite of her disappointment with some of the Society of Friends' individual churches. They also paint a picture of a strong-willed, principled woman who used her voice to amplify the cause of the enslaved in the South.

Much as Frances Ellen Watkins Harper's did, Sarah's opposition to slavery intensified as the South began to ramp up its efforts to catch fugitive slaves. In 1832, she shared with the Female Literary Society of Philadelphia that she had once been more blinded by her privileged upbringing than she was as she stood before them:

> One short year ago, how different were my feelings on the subject of slavery! It is true, the wail of the captive sometimes came to my ear in the midst of my happiness, and caused my heart to bleed for his wrongs; but, alas! the impression was as evanescent as the early cloud and morning dew. I had formed a little world of my own, and cared not to move beyond its precincts. But how was the scene changed when I beheld the oppressor lurking on the border of my own peaceful home! I

saw his iron hand stretched forth to seize me as his prey, and the cause of the slave became my own. I started up, and with one mighty effort threw from me the lethargy which had covered me as a mantle for years; and determined, by the help of the Almighty, to use every exertion in my power to elevate the character of my wronged and neglected race. One year ago, I detested the slaveholder; now I can pity and pray for him. Has not this been your experience, my sisters? Have you not felt as I have felt upon this thrilling subject? My heart assures me some of you have.[16]

In Sarah's speech, we have yet another example of the African American jeremiad, as described by Willie J. Harrell Jr. in *Origins of the African American Jeremiad*:

> Sarah M. Douglass utilized the jeremiad "to stir up in the bosom" of her audience "gratitude to God for his increasing goodness, and feeling of deep sympathy" for the unfortunate souls "in this land of Christian light and liberty held in bondage the most cruel and degrading" ways in the South ("Speech by Sarah M. Douglass" 116).[17]

In spite of Sarah's having been raised by two staunch abolitionists, her response to slavery had to be shaped by her own convictions. And as it was shaped, she added the Female Anti-Slavery Society to her long list of affiliations. She exerted the bulk of her anti-slavery efforts in the teaching of her students, partnering with the Anti-Slavery Society in the running of her school. She continued to write for *The Liberator* and to develop close relationships with white abolitionists like Lucretia Mott, as well as maintaining her close connections with the Forten family.

In 1855, Sarah married William Douglass, a widowed Episcopalian minister, and took on the care of his nine children, pausing her anti-slavery activism. The marriage was brief and not particularly happy, and when it ended with William's death in 1861, Sarah threw herself back into her labors.

By this time, Sarah had left the school she founded and was once more working with the Quakers at the Institute for Colored Youth. She used her medical training to teach courses on hygiene, anatomy, and health to Black women. Throughout the Civil War, she continued fundraising for anti-slavery causes, educating freed Black people in Philadelphia, and teaching.

Sarah Mapps Douglass retired from teaching in 1877. She died five years later.

Legacy and Accountability

I first learned about Sarah Mapps Douglass in the same book that I first read Sara G. Stanley's name—*You Have Stept Out of Your Place: A History of Women and Religion in America*. She was mentioned in a seemingly throwaway line, just like the other Sara, and I remember looking her up then and moving on to different women.

As the book you hold in your hands began to take shape, I found myself stuck on whom to include as the tenth woman. The women in the nine preceding chapters all jumped out at me for different reasons, and seemed easy enough fits for the task at hand. All but Elizabeth Freeman were teachers of some sort—and who is to say what Elizabeth Freeman could have accomplished had she been afforded the same educational opportunities as the rest? All played a pivotal role in establishing Black citizenship in America. All were women who declared an abiding love of the Lord so rich that I cannot wait to spend eternity talking with them as we behold the face of our Savior.

And Sarah Mapps Douglass stands out to me for all of these reasons. She shares a commonality with each and every woman in these pages, the same way that I hope I do—the same way that I hope I will as I continue to grow in grace, maturity, and conviction.

Yet the thing that sets Sarah apart from the rest of these women as I close the ten powerful stories I have been privileged to write—is the courageous way that she spoke truth to power, not on a stage and to America at large, but to the Church. Not to an errant member of the church, the way Sara G. Stanley did—no, she called out the Society of Friends in her area as a whole because of its lack of Christian love displayed to Black Friends.

The Society of Friends had been good to her family. Without them, her ancestor Cyrus Bustill would not have been freed. He would not have learned the trade that afforded his family the comfortable Philadelphia existence that was rare for a Black family. By most accounts, Sarah had very little to complain about. She grew up comfortable and well-educated, and was able to take advantage of myriad opportunities that appeared before her.

It is not difficult to imagine someone pointing out Sarah as a nitpicker. I can just hear some decrying her anger at the Society of Friends as a detraction from all of the good work they were doing. In a time when swaths of white Americans owned Black Americans, forbade them from receiving an education, and did not practice church discipline against white masters who abused their slaves, the Society of Friends decried slavery, worked to set up schools designed to educate freed Black children, and did not allow members to own slaves.

> Sarah spoke truth to power, not on a stage and to America at large, but to the Church.

*Yes, Sarah, it's bad that they made you sit in a segregated part of the church, but can't you just focus on **all of the good they have done**, not just for other Black people in America, but for you?*

Sarah herself had a stint being educated in a Quaker school!

And yet she understood what I hope I understand, even as I look at the history of Presbyterian activism on behalf of my Black kinsmen: we have a higher standard than the status quo. Those Quaker churches that practiced segregation (notably, not all of them did) could not stand before the Lord on judgment day and cite the fact that some Presbyterian churches didn't even let Black people attend their services; they couldn't judge themselves by the cruelty of the cruelest slave master, or the complacency of other believers in the face of discrimination. They could not judge themselves by the lowest common denominator in American society, or even the highest.

They were called to a higher standard than the standard of the land. They were called to the highest standard possible: the standard set forth in the person and work of Jesus Christ. The man whose death, burial, and resurrection struck a death knell to the racial hostilities that warred to define American culture.

Shortly after Sarah Mapps Douglass died, Ida B. Wells critiqued American clergy for their silence in the face of lynching:

> It is the easiest way to get along in the South . . . to ignore the question altogether; our American Christians are too busy saving the souls of white Christians from burning in hell-fire to save the lives of black ones from present burning in fires kindled by white Christians. The feelings of the people who commit these acts must not be hurt by protesting against this sort of thing, and so the bodies of the victims of mob hate must be sacrificed, and the country disgraced because of that fear to speak out.[18]

The activist struggled to see *one* denomination calling out the horror and disgrace of *lynching*—let alone the Jim Crowe laws that facilitated the practice. And yet, there was Sarah, so many years earlier, critiquing a denomination that hadn't been nearly as silent.

Sarah was not content with the Quakers just being "better than" other religious people of the period. Her concern was not in comparing these good white folks to the most racist white folks in other places. Sarah's concern was what was right. And it was not out of disrespect or hatred that she critiqued the Quakers—it was clearly out of love, and a sincere belief that the Society of Friends could be the green pastures that the "poor stray starving sheep, wandering in this world's wilderness" needed.

This is the beauty of loving the Church well: we are called to hold her accountable to the Word, not to the lowest common denominator in the world.

Sarah Mapps Douglass did this well. As did Elizabeth Freeman, Sara Griffith Stanley, Nannie Helen Burroughs, Frances Ellen Watkins Harper, Amanda Berry Smith, Maria Fearing, Maria Stewart, Lucy Craft Laney, and Charlotte Forten Grimké. Even if they did not do it by directly calling out the Church in so many words, they did it by living lives of radical obedience to the Lord in spite of the failings of a country that was supposedly founded on the principles of his Word.

As we strive to make peace with the fact that the evangelical church has not always lived up to God's standard of treatment for Black and brown bodies made in his image, these ten women stand as shining examples of the fact that, even when individual churches or cultural churches fail, the Bride of Christ will prevail through the radical obedience of the remnant.

These ten women were part of that remnant.

And their names should never be forgotten.

The Women I Left Out

The list of women in these pages is completely different than the list of women I started out with. I wanted to write about Fannie Lou Hamer, Mamie Till, Bessie Coleman, Maggie Lena Walker, Sojourner Truth, Fanny Jackson Coppin, and others. And then, the more I researched, the more *other* names started leaping out at me: Mary S. Peake, Charlotte Forten Grimké, Bessie Coleman's aunts Harriet and Sarah Forten Purvis, Lulu Fleming, Blanche Harris, and so many more. Some names I didn't include because I wanted to shed light on some lesser-known sisters. Some names I didn't include because I simply couldn't find enough information on them to share more than a few lines. And for so many others, there just wasn't time or space to tell you everything that I wanted you to know.

I also wanted to make sure I included women of deep faith. While there are so many activists who accomplished so much on behalf of women in general and Black women in particular, not all of them loved Jesus. And of course, even if they did, that might not have been a central aspect of their writing or speaking. Too, because I did not have the privilege of meeting these women, I cannot vouch for the personal fruit of their

169

lives; however, I felt confident that the ten women I listed here could teach readers so much about what it looks like to walk with God.

I cannot speak for the masses here, so I will speak based on my own experience growing up as a minority in white evangelical circles. So often, when it came to unknown Black heroes, the litmus test of whether or not they were "solid" Christians seemed to be more rigorous than their white counterparts. They were viewed with so much theological and doctrinal suspicion, especially if they came from faith traditions different than ours. Black people just weren't "solid," because they often didn't come from Corrie ten Boom's Dutch Reformed tradition or Mary Slessor's Scottish Presbyterian background.

I often felt that I had to be able to poll every Black Christian figure I ran across on very important, weighty matters such as virgin birth or the resurrection, as well as secondary matters such as whether or not women belong in the pulpit. I felt that I had to know the ins and outs of their theological convictions before I could commend them as good and faithful examples in the areas that I *could* know.

And I tended to assume that the more I dug, the more dirt I would find.

> From what I could tell, the women I included lived faithful—though imperfect—lives of service to Jesus.

I did not choose these women because they passed my every theological test. I could not ask them every faith-based question I wanted answered, and they did not write exhaustive commentaries that I can check next to Scripture. But from what I could tell, they lived faithful—though imperfect—lives of service to Jesus, with lessons I was so eager and grateful to mine. The more you sit with them, the more you might find areas of disagreement or imperfection—just as you might with any Christian living today—but their testimonies are overwhelmingly encouraging.

An encouraging testimony I did *not* expect came from Ida B. Wells. She is more well-known than the ten women in this book, but that change has happened in recent years. Ida was a journalist, a civil rights activist, a suffragist, and a force to be reckoned with. And when I started writing this book, I assumed she wouldn't be a candidate for these pages, because she did not write often about her faith (although she did have many critiques for the so-called "Christian" virtues of a lynching South[1]).

But I was wrong. On her twenty-fifth birthday, Ida wrote a journal entry that captures all of the beauty and struggle of trying to live a life set apart for Christ:

> This morning I stand face to face with twenty five years of life, that ere the day is gone will have passed by me forever. The experiences of a quarter of a century of life are my own, beginning with this, for me, new year. Already I stand upon one fourth of the extreme limit (100 years), and have passed one third of the span of life which, according to Psalmist, is allotted to humanity. As this day's arrival enables to me to count the twenty fifth milestone, I go back over them in memory and review my life. The first ten are so far away, in the distance as to make those at the beginning indistinct; the next 5 are remembered as a kind of butterfly existence at school, and household duties at home; within the last ten I have suffered more, learned more, lost more than I ever expect to, again. In the last decade, I've only begun to live—to know life as a whole with its joys and sorrows. . . . [T]here is nothing for which I lament the wasted opportunities as I do my neglect to pick up the crumbs of knowledge that were within my reach. Consequently I find myself at this age as deficient in a comprehensive knowledge as the veriest school-girl just entering the higher course. I heartily deplore the neglect. God grant I may be given firmness of purpose sufficient to essay

& continue its eradication! Thou knowest I hunger & thirst after righteousness & knowledge. O, give me the steadiness of purpose, the will to acquire both. Twenty-five years old today! May another 10 years find me increased in honesty & purity of purpose & motive!"[2]

This is the level of earnest faith that I aspire to. The "firmness of purpose," the "hunger & thirst after righteousness & knowledge," "increased in honesty & purity of purpose & motive." All of these are things I see reflected in the lives of the ten precious women I have been blessed to share with you. Even when I read things from them or about them that made me scratch my head or outright disagree (sweet Nannie comes to mind, but so do Sara and others!), that steadfast purposefulness remained.

I pray that this will be true of me. I pray that it will be true of you. I pray that these lives encourage you to pray to the Father to *make* it true.

Acknowledgments

As ever, I am grateful, first and foremost, to my husband, Phillip. Without him, none of my writing would happen—let alone the book you hold in your hands. His love and support are a constant testament to God's faithfulness in my life.

I am so thankful for my boys. I wrote this book while they climbed all over me, made me break for kisses and snacks, and, in the case of my youngest, grew in my belly. They are the reason for everything I do, and they are the best earthly part of who I am.

On that topic, I am thankful to Sarah Love Crawford for picking up Wynn from K–4 so many days while I was at home trying to make a deadline. She is an amazing friend and neighbor, and truly an unsung hero during this entire process.

I am grateful to my agent, Don Gates, for fielding a rapid succession of excited phone calls as this idea first came to fruition, as well as Patnacia Goodman for matching my excitement. I did not realize I needed an editor who sent me thrilled Marco Polos and excited gifs every time I met a deadline—but I did.

Abena Ansah-Wright and I became friends because of this project. The fact that a ridiculously intelligent Vanderbilt PhD candidate believed in my amateur historian take on these women spurred me on more than she will ever know—as did the deep friendship that I got out of the bargain. Portia Collins is a fierce friend and a woman of incredible faith—so when she read my chapter on Sara G. Stanley and wept, I knew I had undertaken a worthwhile project. Her support has been constant, no matter what time of day I FaceTime. These two were my anchors during this project, and a reminder that the Black girl magic I was writing about is very much alive and well.

Karen Ellis was a confidante, spiritual mother, and cheerleader. I cannot believe my luck at having stumbled into a friendship with this incredible woman, and that she puts up with me. Her mentorship is a constant gift.

My mother-in-law, Ophelia, has been such an anchor during this entire process. She loves my boys so well. And my own mother's enthusiasm for this project from day one warmed my heart.

Collin Huber is my favorite editor. He knows my voice and knows when to push me past my preconceived limits. If he believes in a project, I know we can make it happen.

I am grateful to every single student I had during my nine years of teaching. It is so strange to be releasing a book this fall instead of starting my tenth year. There are too many students to name, and their impact on my life is too great to number. I would name each and every one if I could. But Elizabeth and Allie were the most excited about this project, and it made me smile. I am so excited to see the young women they will become. They made coming to work during a pandemic brighter—always. I'm thankful their mothers raised such sweet daughters. I am thankful to the kids I got to teach two years in a row—in eighth and ninth grade—they made it so hard to say goodbye.

To all of the unwritten names: thank you.

Appendix I

The Founding Fathers and Slavery

The founding fathers themselves held a deep disdain of slavery—even those who owned enslaved people themselves. It is worth stopping to reflect on the fact that the architects of what is often cited as the freest nation in the world made a place in that nation for chattel slavery.

Even when they clearly knew it was wrong.

In fact, in the famed Lincoln-Douglass debates, Lincoln himself cited the founding fathers as detesters of the institution. His assertion is well documented.

George Washington once wrote, "There is not a man living who wishes more sincerely than I do, to see a plan adopted for the abolition of [slavery]."[1] John Adams: "[E]very measure of prudence, therefore, ought to be assumed for the eventual total extirpation of Slavery—from the U.S. . . . . I have, through my

whole life, held the practice of Slavery in such abhorrence."[2]
Benjamin Franklin: "Slavery is such an atrocious debasement
of human nature."[3]

Thomas Jefferson had originally written a scathing passage
about slavery into the Declaration of Independence:

> He has waged cruel war against human nature itself, violat-
> ing its most sacred rights of life and liberty in the persons
> of a distant people who never offended him, captivating &
> carrying them into slavery in another hemisphere or to incur
> miserable death in their transportation thither. This piratical
> warfare, the opprobrium of infidel powers, is the warfare of
> the Christian King of Great Britain. Determined to keep open
> a market where Men should be bought & sold, he has prosti-
> tuted his negative for suppressing every legislative attempt to
> prohibit or restrain this execrable commerce. And that this
> assemblage of horrors might want no fact of distinguished die,
> he is now exciting those very people to rise in arms among us,
> and to purchase that liberty of which he has deprived them,
> by murdering the people on whom he has obtruded them: thus
> paying off former crimes committed again the Liberties of one
> people, with crimes which he urges them to commit against
> the lives of another.[4]

This attempt to place the blame for slavery at the feet of
the English was, perhaps, a response to Englishmen who had
pointed out the irony of America battling for independence
while holding others in bondage.

English Tory Samuel Johnson wrote, "How is it that we hear
the loudest *yelps* for liberty among the drivers of negroes?"[5]
And Thomas Paine asked of Americans, "With what consistency, or decency they complain so loudly of attempts to enslave
them, while they hold so many hundred thousands in slavery?"[6] And Richard Wells, a visiting merchant doing business
in Philadelphia, observed, "Were the colonists as earnest for

the preservation of liberty" as they claimed to be, "they would enter into a virtuous and *perpetual* resolve neither to import, nor to purchase any slaves introduced amongst them."[7]

The founders understood this hypocrisy as well as their critics.

Jefferson again:

> And can the liberties of a nation be thought secure when we have removed their only firm basis, a conviction in the minds of the people that these liberties are of the gift of God? That they are not to be violated but with his wrath? Indeed, I tremble for my country when I reflect that God is just: that his justice cannot sleep for ever.[8]

Often, these quotes are used to exonerate the founding fathers for allowing slavery to continue in their new nation. Surely, they always *meant* for slavery to end. They just had other, more pressing concerns to attend to.

Thomas Jefferson would not only hold enslaved people at his expansive home in Monticello, he would father children with his wife's teenaged half-sister, Sally Hemmings, whom he owned.

George Washington's enslaved workforce would be freed after his death. But before then, when Pennsylvania enacted a law that would set slaves free after six months of residence, Washington started moving his slaves from Philadelphia back to Virginia to cheat the residency requirement.

And Patrick Henry admitted openly that slavery was, for him, a matter of convenience:

> It is not a little surprising that the professors of Christianity, whose chief excellence consists in softening the human heart and in cherishing and improving its finer feelings, should

177

encourage a practice so totally repugnant to the first impressions of right and wrong. What adds to the wonder is that this abominable practice has been introduced in the most enlightened ages. Times, that seem to have pretensions to boast of high improvements in the arts and sciences and refined morality, have brought into general use and guarded by many laws, a species of violence and tyranny which our more rude and barbarous, but more honest, ancestors detested. Is it not amazing that, at a time when the rights of humanity are defined and understood with precision in a country, above all others, fond of liberty, that in such an age and in such a country, we find men professing a religion the most humane, mild, gentle, and generous, adopting a principle as repugnant to humanity as it is inconsistent with the Bible and destructive to liberty? Every thinking, honest man rejects it in speculation; how few in conscientious motives!

Would anyone believe I am master of slaves of my own purchase? I am drawn along by the general inconvenience of living here without them. I will not, I cannot justify it. However culpable my conduct, I will so far pay my devoir to virtue as to own the excellence and rectitude of her precepts and lament my want of conformity to them.[9]

It is not hard to imagine that the man who owned Elizabeth Freeman held these two truths in conflict in his own heart as well: the God-given freedom of the declaration he was signing, along with the reality of the convenience of being a slaveholder.

The African American Jeremiad

In his book *The African American Jeremiad: Appeals for Justice in America*, David Howard-Pitney describes the jeremiad this way:

> American jeremiad is a rhetoric of indignation, expressing deep dissatisfaction and urgently challenging the nation to reform. The term *jeremiad*, meaning a lamentation or doleful complaint, derives from the biblical prophet, Jeremiah, who warned of Israel's fall and the destruction of the Jerusalem temple by Babylonia as punishment for the people's failure to keep the Mosaic covenant. Although Jeremiah denounced Israel's wickedness and foresaw tribulation in the near-term, he also looked forward to the nation's repentance and restoration in a future golden age. A uniquely American version of this rhetorical

tradition has been identified by cultural historians as a major convention of American culture.[1]

As Howard-Pitney aptly observes, Americans are not strangers to religious fervor when it comes to our country. He shares, "Many scholars have held that a national 'civil religion' composed of a shared set of myths, symbols, and rituals underpins American society and seeks to unify its diverse polity into one moral-spiritual community."[2] It is because of this "city on a hill" mentality that the jeremiad—first utilized during the age of the Puritans—proved to be an especially stirring form of address.

These sermons were modeled after the prophet Jeremiah, who was sent by God to warn Israel of her impending doom at the hand of the Babylonians. Instead of being the holy and set-apart nation that God had called it to be, Israel had devolved into idolatry and rampant injustice against the most vulnerable members of her society. As early American Christians often drew parallels between their nation and God's chosen people, their jeremiad proved a natural way to remind early America when she was not living up to the beatific spiritual vision so many held for her.

Introduction

1. Michel Martin, "Slave Bible from the 1800s Omitted Key Passages that Could Incite Rebellion" (NPR, December 9, 2018), https://www.npr.org/2018/12/09/674995075/slave-bible-from-the-1800s-omitted-key-passages-that-could-incite-rebellion.

2. On the capitalization of "Black," I credit W.E.B. Du Bois, who considered "the use of a small letter for the name of twelve million Americans and two hundred million human beings a personal insult." *The Correspondence of W.E.B. Du Bois: Selections, 1877–1934*, vol. 1, ed. Herbert Aptheker (Amherst, MA: University of Massachusetts Press, 1973), 390.

Du Bois was referring to the term *negro*, but I capitalize *Black* in that same spirit. It is a nod to the heritage that unites me to the women in this book—a heritage that cannot be traced back to a specific African ancestor but *has* been written in the survival and thriving of Black people here on America's shores.

3. Isabel Wilkerson, *Caste: The Origins of Our Discontents* (New York: Random House, 2020), 45.

4. Sojourner Truth, *Ain't I a Woman?* (United Kingdom: Penguin Books Limited, 2020) ebook.

5. Malcolm X, excerpt from a speech given on May 22, 1962, in Los Angeles.

Chapter 1: A Midwife at the Birth of a Nation

1. Gianna Melillo, "Racial Disparities Persist in Maternal Morbidity, Mortality and Infant Health," *American Journal of Managed Care*, June

13, 2020, https://www.ajmc.com/view/racial-disparities-persist-in-maternal -morbidity-mortality-and-infant-health.

2. From a transcript of the Sheffield Declaration as printed in *The Massachusetts Spy, Or, Thomas's Boston Journal* (February 18, 1773), https:// constitution.org/2-Authors/bcp/sheffield_declaration.html.

3. Ben Z. Rose, "Stockbridge Slave Mum Bett and Her Appeal for Freedom," in *The Bennington Museum: One of America's Outstanding Regional Museums*, vol. 16 (Bennington, VT: The Bennington Museum, 1971), 19.

4. Rose, "Stockbridge Slave Mum Bett," 19.

5. Henry Louis Gates and Evelyn Brooks Higginbotham, eds., *African American Lives* (New York: Oxford University Press, 2004), 318.

6. Biography.com Editors, "Mum Bett," Biography.com (A&E Networks Television, November 8, 2020), https://www.biography.com/activist/mum-bett.

7. Lin-Manuel Miranda, "The Schuyler Sisters" in *Hamilton*, directed by Thomas Kail (Disney 2020, streamed on Disney+).

8. United States Supreme Court, Roger Brooke Taney, John H. Van Evrie, and Samuel A. Cartwright, *The Dred Scott Decision: Opinion of Chief Justice Taney* (New York: Van Evrie, Horton & Co., 1860), pdf, https://www .loc.gov/item/17001543/.

9. U.S. Supreme Court, *Dred Scott Decision.*

10. Elizabeth Freeman in Gretchen Woelfle, *Answering the Cry for Freedom: Stories of African Americans and the American Revolution* (Homesdale, PA: Calkins Creek, 2016), 73.

Chapter 2: The Almost-Forgotten Spitfire

1. Judith Weisenfeld, "'Who Is Sufficient for These Things?' Sara G. Stanley and the American Missionary Association, 1864–1868," *Church History* 60, no. 4 (1991): 493–507, accessed June 4, 2021, doi:10.2307/3169030.

2. Ellen NicKenzie Lawson, *The Three Sarahs: Documents of Antebellum Black College Women* (New York, NY: E. Mellen Press, 1984), 48.

3. Sara Stanley in her 19 January 1864 application to teach Freedmen in Lawson, *The Three Sarahs,* 78.

4. Further application to teach Freedmen in Lawson, *The Three Sarahs*, 64.

5. Sara G. Stanley, "(1856) Sara G. Stanley Addresses the Convention of Disenfranchised Citizens of Ohio," *Blackpast*, January 24, 2007, accessed October 5, 2019, https://www.blackpast.org/african-american-history/1856 -sara-g-stanley-addresses-convention-disfranchised-citizens-ohio/.

6. Application to teach Freedmen in Lawson, *The Three Sarahs*, 64.

7. "Stanley Addresses the Convention of Disenfranchised."

8. "Stanley Addresses the Convention of Disenfranchised."

9. "Stanley Addresses the Convention of Disenfranchised."

10. Application to teach Freedmen in Lawson, *The Three Sarahs*, 64.

11. Weisenfeld, "Who Is Sufficient for These Things?" 493–507. Accessed January 17, 2021, http://www.jstor.org/stable/3169030.

12. Lawson, *The Three Sarahs*, 64.

13. Daina Ramey Berry and Kali Nicole Gross, *A Black Women's History of the United States* (Boston, MA: Beacon, 2021), 7–8, Kindle.

Chapter 3: The One I Almost Left Out

1. Karen Hunter and Nannie Helen Burroughs, *Stop Being Niggardly: and Nine Other Things Black People Need to Stop Doing* (New York, NY: Gallery Books, 2010), 611, Kindle.

2. Nannie Helen Burroughs and Kelisha B. Graves, *Nannie Helen Burroughs: a Documentary Portrait of an Early Civil Rights Pioneer, 1900–1959* (Notre Dame, IN: University of Notre Dame Press, 2019), 292, Scribd.

3. Burroughs and Graves, *Nannie Helen Burroughs*, 310, Scribd.

4. Burroughs and Graves, *Nannie Helen Burroughs*, 298, Scribd.

5. Burroughs and Graves, *Nannie Helen Burroughs*, 310, Scribd.

6. Malcolm X and Alex Haley, *The Autobiography of Malcolm X: with the Assistance of Alex Haley* (New York, NY: Ballantine Books, 1973), 84.

7. Audrey Thomas McCluskey, *A Forgotten Sisterhood: Pioneering Black Women Educators and Activists in the Jim Crow South* (Lanham, MD: Rowman & Littlefield, 2017), 104.

8. McCluskey, *A Forgotten Sisterhood*, 105.

9. McCluskey, *A Forgotten Sisterhood*, 105.

10. Burroughs and Graves, *Nannie Helen Burroughs*, 95, Scribd.

11. Burroughs and Graves, *Nannie Helen Burroughs*, 253, Scribd.

12. Sadie Iola Daniel, *Women Builders* (Washington, DC: The Associated Publishers, 1931), 104.

13. McCluskey, *A Forgotten Sisterhood*, 107.

14. Burroughs and Graves, *Nannie Helen Burroughs*, 15, Scribd.

15. Burroughs and Graves, *Nannie Helen Burroughs*, 68, Scribd.

16. Burroughs and Graves, *Nannie Helen Burroughs*, 80, Scribd.

17. Burroughs and Graves, *Nannie Helen Burroughs*, 114, Scribd.

Chapter 4: Inspired by the Bronze Muse

1. Bettye J. Gardner, "William Watkins: Antebellum Black Teacher and Anti-slavery Writer," *Negro History Bulletin* 39, no. 6 (1976): 623–25, accessed June 12, 2021, http://www.jstor.org/stable/44175779.

2. Emmanuel S. Nelson, ed., *African American Authors, 1745–1945: Bio-Bibliographical Critical Sourcebook* (Westport, CT: Greenwood Publishing Group, 2000), 214.

3. Elizabeth Ammons and Frances Ellen Watkins [Harper], "Frances Ellen Watkins Harper (1825–1911)," University of Nebraska Press, *Legacy* 2, no. 2 (Fall 1985): 61–66, https://www.jstor.org/stable/25678939.

4. Alice Clark, "Frances Ellen Watkins Harper," *Negro History Bulletin* 5, no. 4 (January 1942): 83, 90, https://www.jstor.org/stable/44246663.

5. Rachel Chang, "How Harriet Tubman and William Still Helped the Underground Railroad," updated Jan 28, 2021, original July 24, 2019, Biography.com, accessed June 16, 2021, https://www.biography.com/news/harriet-tubman-william-still-helped-slaves-escape-underground-railroad.

6. Ammons and Watkins, "Frances Ellen Watkins Harper," 62.

7. Ammons and Watkins, "Frances Ellen Watkins Harper," 60.

8. Frances Ellen Watkins Harper in *Black Women in Nineteenth-Century American Life: Their Words, Their Thoughts, Their Feelings*, ed. Bert James Loewenberg and Ruth Bogin (University Park, PA: Pennsylvania State University Press, 1996), 249.

9. Harper in *Black Women*, 245.

10. Ammons and Watkins, "Frances Ellen Watkins Harper," 64.

11. Frances Harper, *A Brighter Coming Day: A Frances Ellen Watkins Harper Reader*, ed. Frances Foster (New York, NY: Feminist Press, 1990), 296.

12. Harper, *A Brighter Coming Day*, 286.

13. Elizabeth Ammons and Frances Ellen Watkins [Harper], "Frances Ellen Watkins Harper (1825–1911)" *Legacy* 2, no. 2 (1985): 61-66. Accessed June 24, 2021, http://www.jstor.org/stable/25678939.

14. Melba Joyce Boyd, *Discarded Legacy: Politics and Poetics in the Life of Frances E.W. Harper, 1825–1911* (Detroit, MI: Wayne State University Press, 1994), 40.

15. Harper, *A Brighter Coming Day*, 47.

16. Frances Ellen Watkins Harper, *Iola Leroy: or, Shadows Uplifted*, ed. Koritha Mitchell (Ontario, Canada: Broadview Press, 2018), 11–12, Kindle.

17. Frederick Douglass, *Narrative of the Life of Frederick Douglass* (S.l.: Collectors Library, 2022).

18. Harper, *Iola Leroy*, 16, Kindle.

19. Harper, *Iola Leroy*, 32, Kindle.

20. Harper, *Iola Leroy*, 25–26, Kindle.

21. Harper, *Iola Leroy*, 40, Kindle.

Chapter 5: God's Image Carved in Ebony

1. Adrienne M. Israel, *Amanda Berry Smith: From Washerwoman to Evangelist* (Lanham, MD: Scarecrow Press, Inc., 2003), 5.

2. Amanda Smith, *An Autobiography, the Story of the Lord's Dealings with Mrs. Amanda Smith, the Colored Evangelist* (New York, NY: Oxford University Press, 1988), 26.

3. Smith, *An Autobiography*, 117.

4. Smith, *An Autobiography*, 135–136.

5. Smith, *An Autobiography*, 232.

6. Israel, *Amanda Berry Smith*, 53.

7. Kimberly Hill, "Careers Across Color Lines: American Women Missionaries and Race Relations, 1870–1920" (PhD diss., University of North Carolina at Chapel Hill, 2008), 117.

8. Smith, *An Autobiography*, 522.

9. Smith, *An Autobiography*, 246.

10. Smith, *An Autobiography*, 276.

11. Smith, *An Autobiography*, 277.

12. Smith, *An Autobiography*, 367.

13. Israel, *Amanda Berry Smith*, 29.

14. Andy Naselli, "Models of Sanctification," The Gospel Coalition, accessed January 17, 2021, https://www.thegospelcoalition.org/essay/models -of-sanctification/.

15. Israel, *Amanda Berry Smith*, 41.

16. Hill, *Careers Across Color Lines*, 125.

17. Israel, *Amanda Berry Smith*, 127.

18. Israel, *Amanda Berry Smith*, 20–21.

Chapter 6: Mother from Far Away

1. Michael Harbin, "The Manumission of Slaves in Jubilee and Sabbath Years," *Tyndale Bulletin* 63, no. 1 (January 2012): 53–74.

2. Katharine Gerbner, *Christian Slavery Conversion and Race in the Protestant Atlantic World* (Philadelphia, PA: University of Pennsylvania Press, 2018).

3. Alabama Archives: Slave code of 1833, accessed January 17, 2021, https://archives.alabama.gov/teacher/slavery/lesson1/doc1-9.html.

4. Samuel Norvell Lapsley, William H. Sheppard, Althea Brown Edmiston, Julia Lake Kellersberger, *Four Presbyterian Pioneers in Congo: Samuel N. Lapsley, William H. Sheppard, Maria Fearing, Lucy Gantt Sheppard* (Anniston, AL: Offered by the First Presbyterian Church, 1965), 6.

5. Lapsley et al., *Four Presbyterian Pioneers*, 10.

6. Lapsley et al., *Four Presbyterian Pioneers*, 24.

7. Huston, James L. Huston, "Property Rights in Slavery and the Coming of the Civil War," *The Journal of Southern History* 65, no. 2 (1999): 249-86, accessed June 4, 2021, doi:10.2307/2587364. The use of the word *protection* here should not be confused with its use in the context of something cherished or prized, but rather protected *as property would be protected* under the law.

8. Adam Hochschild, *King Leopold's Ghost: A Story of Greed, Terror, and Heroism in Colonial Africa* (Boston, MA: Mariner Books, 2020), 202.

9. Hochschild, *King Leopold's Ghost*, 135.

10. Lapsley et al., *Four Presbyterian Pioneers*, 28.

11. Lapsley et al., *Four Presbyterian Pioneers*, 31.

12. Karen Yvette Dace, "African-American Christian Female Missionaries in Nyasaland, Congo, and Liberia: Perpetuation and Resistance at the Intersections of Blackness, Gender, Disability, and Christianity" (EdD diss., The University of San Francisco, 2019), 88–91.

13. Dace, "African-American Christian Female Missionaries," 88.

14. Dace, "African-American Christian Female Missionaries," 90.

Chapter 7: Where Are Our Illustrious Ones?

1. David Walker, *Walker's Appeal, in Four Articles; Together with a Preamble, to the Coloured Citizens of the World, but in Particular, and Very Expressly, to Those of the United States of America, Written in Boston, State of Massachusetts, September 28, 1829*, 3, accessed January 17, 2021, https://docsouth.unc.edu/nc/walker/walker.html.

2. Walker, *Walker's Appeal*, 7.

3. Walker, *Walker's Appeal*, 12.

4. Walker, *Walker's Appeal*, 80, 45.

5. Maria Stewart, "Religion and the Pure Principles of Morality: The Sure Foundation on Which We Must Build," speech to free black people in Boston in 1831, *Teaching American History*, accessed January 17, 2021, https://teachingamericanhistory.org/library/document/religion-and-the-pure -principles-of-morality-the-sure-foundation-on-which-we-must-build/.

6. Walker, *Walker's Appeal*, 49.

7. Maria Stewart in *Black Women in Nineteenth-Century American Life: Their Words, Their Thoughts, Their Feelings*, ed. Bert James Loewenberg and Ruth Bogin (University Park, PA: Pennsylvania State University Press, 1996), 197–198.

8. Maria W. Stewart, "Religion and the Pure Principles of Morality, the Sure Foundation on Which We Must Build" in *Productions of Mrs. Maria W. Stewart Presented to the First African Baptist Church & Society, of the City of Boston* (Boston: Friends of Freedom and Virtue, 1835), 3, electronic edition prepared by the New York Public Library, https://s3.amazonaws.com/nypl-aaww /SCAAWW_book_33_Productions_of_Mrs_Maria_W_Stewart_presented_to _the_First_Africa_Baptist_Church_and_Society_of_the_City_of_Boston.pdf.

9. Willie J. Harrell Jr., *Origins of the African American Jeremiad: The Rhetorical Strategies of Social Protest and Activism, 1760–1861* (Jefferson, NC: McFarland, 2011), loc. 1435–1437, Kindle.

10. Stewart, *Productions*, 10.

11. Stewart, *Productions*, 8.

12. Stewart, *Productions*, 4.

13. Stewart, "An Address Delivered at the African Masonic Hall, Boston" in *Productions*, 68.

Chapter 8: A Refined Negro Woman

1. The American Missionary Association is the same Presbyterian-funded ministry that sent Sarah G. Stanley and other black teachers south after the Civil War.

2. There is a yearly meeting for elected commissioners of the Presbyterian church, where important matters of doctrine and practice for the denomination are discussed.

3. Sadie Iola Daniel, *Women Builders* (Washington, DC: The Associated Publishers, 1931), 6.

4. Daniel, *Women Builders*, 12–13.

5. Jennifer Lund Smith, "Lucy Craft Laney and Martha Berry" in *Georgia Women: Their Lives and Times, Volume 1* (Southern Women: Their Lives and Times) ed., Ann Short Chirhart and Betty Wood (Athens, GA: University of Georgia Press, 2009), 323.

6. Audrey Thomas McCluskey, "'We Specialize in the Wholly Impossible': Black Women School Founders and Their Mission." *Signs* 22, no. 2 (1997): 403–426. Accessed January 17, 2021, http://www.jstor.org/stable/3175282.

7. Kent Anderson Leslie, "Lucy Craft Laney (1854-1933)," New Georgia Encyclopedia, updated July 20, 2020, accessed June 17, 2021, https://www .georgiaencyclopedia.org/articles/education/lucy-craft-laney-1854-1933.

8. Audrey Thomas McCluskey, *A Forgotten Sisterhood: Pioneering Black Women Educators and Activists in the Jim Crow South* (Lanham, MD: Rowman & Littlefield, 2017), 17, Kindle.

9. Daniel, *Women Builders*, 7–8.

10. Interestingly, Lucy would rub shoulders with Booker T. Washington, Nannie Helen Burroughs, and W.E.B. DuBois during her career.

11. "(1899) Lucy Craft Laney, 'The Burden of the Educated Colored Woman,'" *BlackPast*, January 29, 2007, accessed June 12, 2020, https://www.black past.org/african-american-history/1899-lucy-craft-laney-burden-educated -colored-woman/.

12. "Lucy Craft Laney," *BlackPast*.

13. A.W. Geiger, "Public School Teachers Are Far Less Racially and Ethnically Diverse Than Their Students," Pew Research Center, PewResearch.org, August 27, 2018, https://www.pewresearch.org/fact-tank/2018/08/27/americas-public -school-teachers-are-far-less-racially-and-ethnically-diverse-than-their-students.

14. Smith, "Lucy Craft Laney and Martha Berry" in *Georgia Women*, 318.

15. Smith, "Lucy Craft Laney and Martha Berry" in *Georgia Women*, 327–328.

16. Daniel, *Women Builders*, 21–22.

17. Daniel, *Women Builders*, 22.

18. Smith, "Lucy Craft Laney and Martha Berry" in *Georgia Women*, 328.

Chapter 9: Daughter of a Legacy

1. Julie Winch, "'You Know I Am a Man of Business': James Forten and the Factor of Race in Philadelphia's Antebellum Business Community," *Business and Economic History* 26, no. 1 (1997): 213-28. Accessed June 24, 2021, http://www.jstor.org/stable/23703308.

2. "Grimké, Charlotte Forten" in Philip Bader, *African American Writers* (New York: Facts on File, 2004), 104.

3. Winch, "You Know I Am a Man of Business."

4. Willie J. Harrell Jr., *Origins of the African American Jeremiad: The Rhetorical Strategies of Social Protest and Activism, 1760–1861* (Jefferson, NC: McFarland, 2011), loc. 463–464, Kindle.

5. Charlotte Forten, *A Free Black Girl before the Civil War: The Diary of Charlotte Forten, 1854*, ed. Christy Steele (Mankato, MN: Capstone, 2000), 26.

6. "Journal of Charlotte Forten: Free Woman of Color," *The Making of African American Identity: Vol. I, 1500–1865*, Primary Resources in U.S. History and Literature, Toolbox Library, National Humanities Center, accessed January 17, 2021, http://nationalhumanitiescenter.org/pds/maai/index .htm.

7. Charlotte L. Forten, *The Journals of Charlotte Forten Grimké*, ed. Brenda E. Stevenson (New York: Oxford University Press, 1988), 65-66.

8. "Living Contraband," National Parks Service, U.S. Department of the Interior, accessed August 15, 2017, https://www.nps.gov/articles/living -contraband-former-slaves-in-the-nation-s-capital-during-the-civil-war .htm.

9. "Charlotte Forten Grimké," National Park Service, U.S. Department of the Interior, accessed July 5, 2020, https://www.nps.gov/people/charlotte -forten-grimke.htm.

10. Charlotte Forten, "Life on the Sea Islands (Part I)," *Atlantic Monthly*, May 1864, https://www.theatlantic.com/magazine/archive/1864/05/life-on -the-sea-islands/308758/.

11. Forten, "Life on the Sea Islands."

12. Francis James Grimké, *Meditations on Preaching* (Madison, MS: Log College Press, 2018), 2.

Chapter 10: She Leaned upon the Rock of Ages

1. Oliver S. Heckman, "The Presbyterian Church in the United States of America in Southern Reconstruction, 1860–1880." *The North Carolina Historical Review* 20, no. 3 (1943): 219–237. Accessed January 16, 2021, http://www.jstor.org/stable/23515237.

2. Mark Andrew Huddle, "Quaker Abolitionists," NCpedia (Tar Heel Junior Historian, NC Museum of History, Fall, 1996), https://www.ncpedia .org/culture/religion/quaker-abolitionists.

3. "North Carolina Quakers Fight Against Slavery," *The History Engine*, Digital Scholarship Lab, 2008, https://historyengine.richmond.edu/episodes /view/3852.

4. Anna Bustill Smith, "The Bustill Family" in *The Journal of Negro History* 10, no. 4 (October 1925): 638–644, accessed January 16, 2021, https:// www.journals.uchicago.edu/doi/10.2307/2714143.

5. Valerie D. Levy, "Sarah Mapps Douglass," *Voices from the Gaps*, Regents of the University of Minnesota, 2009, https://conservancy.umn .edu/bitstream/handle/11299/166156/Douglass,%20Sarah%20Mapps .pdf?sequence=1&isAllowed=y.

6. Tabitha A. Morgan, "Revolution and Roses: The Voice and Aesthetic of Sarah Mapps Douglass," *Pennsylvania History: A Journal of Mid-Atlantic*

Studies 87, no. 4 (Autumn 2020): 657–663, accessed January 16, 2021, https://www.jstor.org/stable/10.5325/pennhistory.87.4.0657.

7. Morgan, "Revolution and Roses."

8. Rebecca Bayeck, "Robert Douglass Jr., 19th Century African American Artist," The New York Public Library, May 22, 2020, https://www.nypl.org/blog/2020/05/22/robert-douglass-jr-african-american-artist.

9. Margaret Malamud, *African Americans and the Classics: Antiquity, Abolition and Activism* (London: I.B. Tauris, 2019), 66.

10. Mary Kelley, "'Talents Committed to Your Care': Reading and Writing Radical Abolitionism in Antebellum America," *The New England Quarterly* 88, no. 1 (March 2015): 37–72, accessed January 16, 2021, http://www.jstor.org/stable/24718202.

11. Margaret Hope Bacon, "New Light on Sarah Mapps Douglass and Her Reconciliation with Friends," *Quaker History* 90, no. 1 (Spring 2001): 28–49. Accessed January 16, 2021, http://www.jstor.org/stable/41947773.

12. Bacon, "New Light," 32.

13. Bacon, "New Light," 32.

14. Jasmine L. Holmes, *Mother to Son: Letters to a Black Boy on Identity and Hope* (Downers Grove, IL: IVP, an imprint of InterVarsity Press, 2020), 74–75, 96.

15. Bacon, "New Light," 33.

16. "(1832) Sarah Mapps Douglas Urges Support for the Anti-Slavery Cause," *Blackpast*, September 22, 2008, https://www.blackpast.org/african-american-history/1832-sarah-mapps-douglas-urges-support-anti-slavery-cause/.

17. Willie J. Harrell Jr., *Origins of the African American Jeremiad: The Rhetorical Strategies of Social Protest and Activism, 1760–1861* (Jefferson, NC: McFarland, 2011), loc. 412, Kindle.

18. Ida B. Wells, *The Crusade for Justice: The Autobiography of Ida B. Wells,* second edition, ed. Alfreda M. Duster (Chicago, IL: University of Chicago Press, 1970, 2020), 131.

The Women I Left Out

1. Ida B. Wells, *Crusade for Justice: The Autobiography of Ida B. Wells*, ed. Alfreda M. Duster (Chicago, IL: University of Chicago Press, 1970), 154–155.

2. Ida B. Wells in Michelle Duster, *Ida B. the Queen: The Extraordinary Life and Legacy of Ida B. Wells* (New York: Atria/One Signal Publishers, 2021), Kindle.

Appendix I: The Founding Fathers and Slavery

1. "From George Washington to Robert Morris, 12 April 1786," *Founders Online*, National Archives, https://founders.archives.gov/documents/Washington/04-04-02-0019. Original source: *The Papers of George Washington, Confederation Series*, vol. 4, 2 April 1786–31 January 1787, ed. W.W. Abbot (Charlottesville: University Press of Virginia, 1995), 15–17.

2. "From John Adams to Robert J. Evans, 8 June 1819," *Founders Online*, National Archives, https://founders.archives.gov/documents/Adams/99-02 -02-7148. This is an Early Access document from *The Adams Papers*, not an authoritative final version.

3. Pennsylvania Society for Promoting the Abolition of Slavery, "An Address to the Public, from the Pennsylvania Society for Promoting the Abolition of Slavery, and the Relief of Free Negroes, Unlawfully Held in Bondage . . . Signed by order of the Society, B. Franklin, President," (Philadelphia, November 9, 1789), PDF, https://www.loc.gov/item/2005577131/.

4. "(1776) The Deleted Passage of the Declaration of Independence," *BlackPast*, https://www.blackpast.org/african-american-history /declaration-independence-and-debate-over-slavery/. Original source: Thomas Jefferson, *The Writings of Thomas Jefferson: Being His Autobiography, Correspondence, Reports, Messages, Addresses, and other Writings, Official and Private* (Washington, D.C.: Taylor & Maury, 1853–1854).

5. Hugh Thomas, *The Slave Trade: The Story of the Atlantic Slave Trade: 1440–1870*, (New York: Simon & Schuster, 1997), 467.

6. Thomas Paine, *The Writings of Thomas Paine*, ed. Moncure Daniel Conway, vol. 1. 1774–1779 (London: G.P. Putnam's Sons, 1894), 7.

7. Douglas R. Egerton, *Death or Liberty: African Americans and Revolutionary America* (Oxford: Oxford University Press, 2009), 51.

8. Thomas Jefferson, *Notes on the State of Virginia*, 1781, American Studies at the University of Virginia, hypertext, http://xroads.virginia.edu /~Hyper/JEFFERSON/ch18.html.

9. Harlow G. Unger, *Lion of Liberty: Patrick Henry and the Call to a New Nation* (Cambridge, MA: Da Capo Press, 2011), 238, Kindle.

Appendix II: The African American Jeremiad

1. David Howard-Pitney, *African American Jeremiad: Appeals for Justice in America, Revised and Expanded Edition* (Philadelphia: Temple University Press, 1998) loc. 85–89, Kindle.

2. Howard-Pitney, *African American Jeremiad*, loc. 85–89, Kindle.

Jasmine L. Holmes is the author of *Mother to Son: Letters to a Black Boy on Identity and Hope*. She is also a contributing author for *Identity Theft: Reclaiming the Truth of Our Identity in Christ* and *His Testimonies, My Heritage: Women of Color on the Word of God*. She and her husband, Phillip, are parenting three young sons in Jackson, Mississippi.